# Home Sausage Making

# Home Sausage Making

## REVISED EDITION

BY
CHARLES G. REAVIS

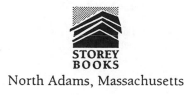

STOREY
BOOKS
North Adams, Massachusetts

*The mission of Storey Communications is to serve our customers by publishing practical information that encourages personal independence in harmony with the environment.*

## This book is dedicated to my family, of course.

Front cover art by Loretta Trezzo Braren
Drawings by Sue Storey
Photography by Erik Borg
Typesetting by Jackson Typesetters
Designed and produced by Nancy M. Lamb & Wanda Harper
Edited by Constance L. Oxley
© Copyright 1987 by Storey Communications, Inc.

The information in this book is true and complete to the best of our knowledge. All recommendations are made without guarantee on the part of the author or Storey Books. The author and publisher disclaim any liability in connection with the use of this information. For additional information, please contact Storey Books, 210 MASS MoCA Way, North Adams, MA 01247.

Storey Books are available for special premium and promotional uses and for customized editions. For further information, please call Storey's Custom Publishing Department at 1-800-793-9396.

*Printed in the United States by Capital City Press*
*30  29  28  27  26  25  24  23  22  21  20*

**Library of Congress Catalog Card Number: 87-045094**
**International Standard Book Number: 0-88266-477-8**

**Library of Congress Cataloging-in-Publication Data**

Reavis, Charles, 1948–
    Home sausage making.

    Bibliography: p.
    Includes index.
    1. Sausages    2. Cookery (Sausages)    I. Title.
TX749.R4    1987          641.6'6          87-45094
ISBN 0-88266-477-8

# Contents

# Acknowledgments

I would like to thank several people who helped me revise and update *Home Sausage Making, Revised Edition.* First of all, I would like to thank the knowledgeable people at the Broome County, New York, Division of Cooperative Extension. If they didn't have the answers to my questions, they at least pointed me in the right direction. Also, the office of Congressman Matthew McHugh of New York was helpful in obtaining information about the nitrite/nitrate question from the Food and Drug administration. Furthermore, I would like to thank Professor John N. Sofos of the Colorado State University Department of Animal Sciences who was kind enough to supply me with much of the latest scientific information about processed meats and their preservation.

A special thanks is due the friendly people of the Cooperative Extension Division at Cornell University and especially Professor Robert Baker, Chairman of the Poultry Science Department. Professor Baker, also known as the "Father of the Chicken Dog," was generous with his time and patience in answering my questions about poultry and fish sausages. I would be remiss if I didn't say thank you to my editor on this book, Connie Oxley, the guardian of good grammar and spelling. Lastly, I must say thanks to my family for putting up with me and without me during the last few months.

# Introduction

Sausage making is one of the (almost) lost arts, but one that is gaining in popularity. When you have smelled a batch of homemade, plump, juicy sausages sizzling on a grill in your own kitchen, you will appreciate the thrill and satisfaction that comes with making your own.

Making your own sausage is easy: I'll show you how.

Making your own sausage is economical: you can use cheaper cuts of meat that you might not ordinarily consider buying. Alternatively, if you have the land and the time, you can raise your own meat and reduce the cost of your sausage even further. And, of course, there is always the opportunity to hunt for some of your own meat much like your ancestors did. Wild game meats make fine sausage.

Making your own sausage is fun; you'll relish the satisfaction that comes from turning out plump, juicy sausages with your own hands.

Making your own sausage is, best of all, better for you. You know exactly what goes into it, and the conditions under which you make it are as clean and wholesome as you care to make them.

Since the preceding words were written over five years ago, people have become even more health conscious, more attentive to what they put into their bodies. Increasing awareness of the deleterious effects of too much salt or fat in the diet has led many people to radically change their eating habits, often to the extent of forsaking foods that once were considered dietary staples.

Gorging is out; grazing is in.

The answer to the question "Where's the beef?" is increasingly "home on the range" and not on the dinner plate.

While most nutrition advocates recommend a change in eating habits that reflect a lower fat and salt intake and less reliance on protein and a greater reliance on the complex carbohydrates, most of them also stress that the key to healthful eating is *moderation.* One need not give up completely foods that one enjoys to maintain a healthful lifestyle. Often minor adjustments in food preparation, ingredients, and eating patterns are all that is needed to become a "smart" eater.

Sausages have traditionally been thought of as fatty food. Indeed, the reputation is not wholly undeserved. If you were to fry down a batch of many commercially prepared sausages, you would undoubtedly find that more often than not, they contain more fat and water than they do meat. This need not be the case, however, when you make your own sausage. Furthermore, the traditional sausage meats, mainly pork and beef, are not the only meats suited to making a good sausage. As the earlier edition of this book pointed out, veal and game meats which are naturally lower in fat content, are also well suited to making sausage.

In this new edition of *Home Sausage Making*, we will explore even newer ways of making sausage, using poultry and fish. As far as the more traditional sausages are concerned, minor adjustments in fat and salt content can very well spell the difference between a "no-no" food and one that can be enjoyed in moderation without feeling guilty about wreaking havoc with one's body.

All the original reasons we discussed in the beginning of this introduction for making one's own sausage are just as true and valid today as they were five years ago, probably even more so.

Happy sausage making!

# The Many Sausages

**M**aking your own sausage will put you in a league with some famous people who, even if they didn't actually make their own, contributed to sausage's sometimes inglorious past.

Although Homer didn't mention anything about Helen of Troy sending out for a sausage and pepperoni pizza, he did state in the *Odyssey* that when the Greeks and Trojans weren't fighting, they often enjoyed a few plump well-turned sausages grilled over the campfire.

Constantine, on the other hand, banned sausage shortly after he inherited the Roman Empire. It seems that he was embarrassed by the orgies at which sausage was often consumed. His puritanical sensibilities simply wouldn't stand for it. Of course, he also banned skinny-dipping in the public baths, so you know that he was just no fun at all.

Our own history might have been different if (so the story goes) Captain John Smith hadn't been so adept at roasting his homemade kielbasa over an open fire. It seems that Pocahontas loved that sausage, and so she convinced daddy to spare Captain John's life. And they say the way to a *man's* heart . . . ? Anyway, with a name like Smith, it was no easy feat for kielbasa to come to the rescue.

Apocryphal? Maybe. But you get the idea.

# Sausage Varieties

To the best of my knowledge, no one has ever catalogued all the various kinds of sausages in the world. The attempt would probably be futile anyway since some sausage is made only in a small region, and some kinds of sausage don't even exist anymore. The American Indians, for example, made several kinds of dried or cured sausages from meat and berries, but they never bothered to write down their recipes. To further complicate matters, every sausage maker has his own (very often secret) recipe for a particular kind of sausage. A generic

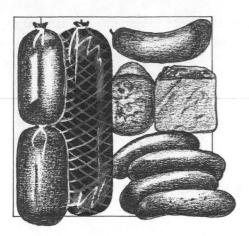

term like "salami" refers to dozens of different sausages, some no more alike than night and day.

It is for these reasons that there really is no such thing as "Italian sausage" or "Polish sausage" or any of the other dozens of ethnic varieties sold in most supermarkets. Certain *kinds* of sausages owe allegiance to various countries or regions but "Italian sausage" may be Italian to one person, but pure bologna to another.

By definition (mine), sausage is a mixture of ground meat laced with herbs and spices. That doesn't begin to describe the virtually limitless varieties of sausage. Since the first edition of this book was first published, the sausage horizon has been pushed back even further to include varieties made from fresh poultry and fish.

All sausages fall into one of two groups. Fresh sausages must be cooked before being eaten. They must be treated like other fresh meat—kept cold when stored. Cured sausages are preserved with certain ingredients such as salt, and they may have been dried to prevent spoilage. (See Chapter 6 for a discussion of methods of preservation.) Cured sausage can be eaten as is, or with only enough cooking to heat it through.

Let's take a look at the various kinds of sausages we'll be making.

# Fresh Sausages

*Bockwurst* is a German-style sausage made from veal or veal and pork. It is usually flavored with onions, parsley, and cloves.

*Bratwurst* is another German-style sausage made from pork and veal. It looks like a fat hot dog and is delicately flavored with allspice, caraway, and marjoram.

*Country sausage* is one of the most common kinds of sausage found in this country. It can be made into patties or small links and is spiced predominantly with sage.

*Frankfurter*, or your plain old-fashioned hot dog, is the most widely consumed sausage in the world, thanks primarily to the industriousness of American meat packers. Americans consumed 20 *billion* hot dogs in 1985. Though the commercial variety frank sometimes deserves its lowly reputation, consisting as it does of mostly water and fat, the homemade variety belongs on the same pedestal with all the other homemade sausages because it is just as wholesome and delicious.

*Liverwurst* is, next to the hot dog, the most famous of the German-style sausages.

*Vienna* sausage consists primarily of pork and beef, but veal can be added to give it a milder flavor. Onions, mace, and coriander are the predominant flavors.

*Cotechino* is an Italian-style sausage that is best made from fresh, uncured ham. Nutmeg, cinnamon, and cloves combine with Parmesan cheese to give it its unique flavor.

*Luganega* is a very mild Italian-style sausage. It is unique in that it is flavored with freshly grated orange and lemon zest.

*Northern Italian-style* hot or sweet sausage is what you usually see in the meat case labeled simply "Italian sausage." It is traditionally a pure pork sausage in which coriander is the principal herb used in flavoring.

*Sicilian-style* is basically the same as Northern Italian-style sausage except that fennel takes the place of coriander.

*Chorizo* can be either fresh or cured. The fresh variety is similar to Sicilian sausage except that it is much spicier. It is not for people with timid palates.

*Garlic* sausage can also be fresh or cured. The fresh variety is a pork sausage with lots of garlic and a little white wine for flavor. It is an excellent addition to stews or casseroles that call for some sausage because it is able to stand up to long cooking without losing its flavor.

*Polish kielbasa.* Like "Italian sausage," kielbasa is more of a generic term than a reference to a specific sausage. The commercial variety is preserved and pre-cooked, but the homemade variety is just as often made fresh. Although some people are under the impression that kielbasa is made strictly from pork, the fact of the matter is that it can be made from any combination of pork, beef, or veal. Using all three varieties of meat gives the sausage a much more exciting flavor.

# Cured Sausages

Cured sausages would take up the most space in any sausage catalogue. The proliferation of this species is due in part to the imaginations of commercial meat-packing plants' public relations departments. Old time sausage makers were imaginative, to be sure, but the technological *wurstmachers* of today never seem to tire of inventing new varieties—or at least new names for old sausages.

Here are some of the cured sausages we'll be making:

*Pepperoni* is an Italian-style sausage made from beef and pork. It is quite dry and can be extremely pungent depending upon how much red pepper you dare to throw in.

*Salami* is a generic term that refers to sausages made from beef or pork or both. It comes in many shapes and sizes and can be quite hard and dry.

*Garlic sausage*, the cured variety, is an extremely complex combination of flavors. It is not meant to be used in recipes calling for garlic sausage (that province rests with the fresh variety), but is intended to be eaten out of hand.

*Summer sausage*, sometimes called *cervelat*, beefstick or beer sausage, is a beef and pork sausage (or sometimes strictly beef) that resembles some of the drier salamis but has a milder and somewhat sweeter flavor.

*Chorizo* (the dried variety) most closely resembles pepperoni in size and shape but is much more pungent.

*Venison* sausage is one you'll have to hunt for and your grocer's meatcase probably won't have it. It usually includes some pork because venison tends to be a very dry meat.

*Thuringer* sausage is a German-style lightly smoked sausage which, though technically cured, is not extremely dry and is more perishable than other cured sausages. Mace, mustard seed, and coriander provide the flavor.

*Garlic ring bologna* is another "almost cured" sausage that is lightly smoked, pre-cooked, and quite garlicky.

*Mettwurst* is similar in most respects to garlic ring bologna but is milder in flavor. It contains ginger, celery seed, and allspice.

*Braunschweiger* is a pure pork German-style sausage. Its flavor is mild and smoky and accented by onions, mustard seed, and marjoram.

*Smoked country-style sausage* is something you've no doubt encountered in the meat case labeled "little smokies" or something similar. You can easily make your own with pork and beef.

*Smoked kielbasa* is the sausage you will find in the meat case labeled "Polish sausage." It is similar to the fresh variety except that the flavors are more intense because it is smoked and pre-cooked.

*Bavarian summer sausage* is a German-style salami which is indebted to me for its name because whenever I have some I can't help but think of Bavarian beer fests and rye bread. It is very mildly flavored with mustard seed and sugar.

*Yirtrničky* is a Czech sausage most easily made if you have access to freshly butchered pork because its ingredients include the meat from a pig's head along with the lungs, heart, and kidneys.

# The New Sausages

Although inventing a new recipe is much like reinventing the wheel, there really *is* something new in the kitchen. Various descriptions abound, including the term "nouvelle cuisine," but basically what they all amount to is a lighter, more health-conscious way of preparing food.

Together we are going to experiment with our own "nouvelle sausages," and in the process cut down on fats, calories, and cholesterol. Both poultry and fish contain fat, to be sure, but they are lower in fat than beef and pork. Fish, as a matter of fact, contain an entirely different kind of fat, which some studies indicate may actually help to protect against the kinds of illnesses (such as heart disease and cancer) that high fat diets are normally associated with. We'll talk more in Chapter 3 about the health implications of fat and salt in the diet, but in the mean time, suffice it to say that we can have our sausage and our health, too.

# Chapter 2

# Equipment and Ingredients

**T**he French have a term for culinary preparedness: *mise en place.* This means that you should have everything gathered together and "in its place" before you start any recipe. Fortunately you probably already have the equipment you will need, with possibly one or two exceptions, in your kitchen.

# Grinders

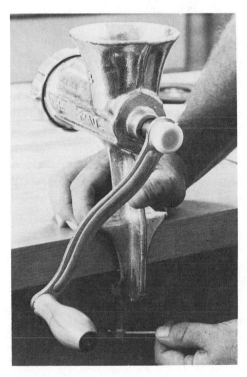

*My grinder gets a firm grip on our kitchen counter.*

Unless you are a graduate of the Japanese Culinary Institute and are able to wield two razor-sharp knives like a samurai warrior (without losing any fingers in the process), you are going to need something with which to grind the meat. Devices for accomplishing this task range from the simple to the exotic, from dirt cheap to dearly expensive.

An old fashioned hand grinder, like the one in your grandmother's kitchen is still a bargain even at today's inflated prices. A good one, with fine and coarse chopping disks, costs less than $25.

A word of caution about the newer plastic hand grinders that can be found in discount stores or ordered from the eternally ubiquitous television commercials (along with the "Vegetable Destroyer" and "The Knife that Never Dies"). The plastic models do look prettier than their cast iron cousins, but they are no where nearly as sturdy. Furthermore, while the metal grinders clamp onto a table edge, the plastic models usually feature a suction cup base. This type of arrangement is generally inferior to the clamp on variety. Grinding meat by hand is the most arduous task of the home sausage maker. A suction cup base can lose its grip at the most inappropriate times. Don't compound the difficulty of an already laborious task by using a grinder that has to be reattached and repositioned every five minutes.

The old metal grinders are still readily available in hardware stores and gourmet cooking supply shops and are virtually indestructible. Ours has been in the family for more than four generations. If you already own a hand grinder, or want to get into sausage making via the last expensive route, an old-fashioned cast iron food grinder will serve you well.

If you do decide to purchase a hand grinder, there are certain things that you should look for. Make sure that the grinder comes with at least two chopping disks: a fine disk, with holes about an eighth of an inch in diameter, and a coarse disk, with holes at least three-eights of an inch in diameter. Look for a model with a heavy duty screw clamp for attaching to a table or countertop. It's better to spend a couple of extra dollars in the beginning for a quality appliance than to regret not doing so later on when the base collapses while grinding a batch of meat.

# Power Grinders

If you don't want to expend the elbow grease to grind meat by hand, an electric food grinder is a wise investment. Expect to pay more. Forty dollars is about rock bottom, with professional models costing as much as $400 or $500. Again, choose one that has at least two cutting disks. Some of the more inexpensive models have motors that are apt to overheat when grinding large batches of meat. Generally speaking, the more expensive the unit, the more powerful the motor.

The Oster Heavy Duty Food Grinder (Model 940-08A) is an excellent choice for the home sausage maker. It comes with fine, medium, and coarse disks, and a sausage making kit is available for an additional five dollars or so that includes an extra coarse disk which is perfect for making larger sausages, as well as three sausage stuffing tubes (small for hot dog sized sausages, medium for Italian-style or similar sausages, and large for salami-style sausages. The Oster Heavy Duty Food Grinder sells for about $60 to $80.

If you are a serious cook, you probably already own a food processor. If you do, you already know that it can do a splendid job for chopping meat. With your food processor all you need is a sausage funnel (see below) and you're in business.

The major drawback with using a food processor is that until one learns the technique involved, it is very easy to over process everything. A few seconds too many, and a pound of one-inch meat cubes is reduced to something resembling toothpaste.

If you already own a food processor, by all means use it for making sausage. If you have considered purchasing one in the near future, here are some things you should look for.

*Here are four sizes of disks commonly used in making sausage.*

Make sure that the unit you choose has a powerful motor. The stronger the motor, the less it has to work, and therefore the longer it should last. A small motor may have to strain at some chopping tasks and runs the risk of overheating and burning out. I know from personal experience that the lower priced food processors (in the $50 to $100 range) tend to self-destruct even after a few months of use.

Look for a model that has a large feed tube. Trying to feed food into some of the smaller models is laborious because of the small opening in the feed tube.

Check the warranty. The larger, more expensive models have twenty or thirty year warranties on the motor: an indication that the manufacturer believes that the motor is up to the challenge of doing what it is supposed to do.

My personal choice in a food processor, and that of many chefs in professional kitchens, is the Cuisinart DLC7PRO. It is a workhorse in the kitchen, capable of doing much more than simply grinding meat. If you are a serious cook, give the DLC7PRO serious consideration. It lists for about $300, but is widely available at a discount.

Other models which are worthy of your consideration and with which I have a passing acquaintance are the Kitchen-Aid KFP700 and the Robot Coupe RC2800-GO. They retail for about as much as the Cuisinart but are also generally available at a discount.

# Sausage Funnel

If your grinder doesn't have a sausage stuffing attachment or you use a food processor to grind your meat, you will need a sausage funnel to stuff the meat into the casings. An ordinary kitchen funnel doesn't have an opening large enough to allow the ground meat to pass through easily. The taper is also such that it doesn't allow you to gather enough casing at one time to be practical. Sausage funnels come in various sizes and can usually be found in butcher supply stores, restaurant supply stores, or can be mail ordered. Regardless of where you happen to find one, the good news is that they are relatively cheap; expect to pay less than $2.

*Old-fashioned but still very practical is this sausage stuffer.*

# Knives

*My preference is a carbon steel knife. I can sharpen it to perfection with my butcher's steel.*

The most universal kitchen/cooking utensil is the knife. It is the single most important piece of equipment you will be using to make sausage because so much of the job involves cutting, boning, and trimming the meat that will be ground into your sausage. The best tool is a knife that can be honed to a razor's edge.

There are four kinds of knives on the market: high carbon steel, carbon steel, stainless steel, and the weapons advertised on television that are supposedly as adept at slicing tomatoes as they are at cutting through tin cans. Aside from the latter, which I consider more a curiosity than a serious culinary tool, let's take a look at what's available and the relative merits of each.

Stainless steel knives are the most popular, easiest to keep clean, and always look shiny. Manufacturers contend that stainless steel knives stay sharp longer. This is probably true, but once it loses its edge, it takes a professional knife sharpener to restore it. A stainless steel knife is my last choice for cutting up in the kitchen.

Carbon steel knives can be honed to an edge sharp enough to shave with. Because carbon steel is not as hard as stainless steel, these knives lose their edge much more rapidly than their stainless cousins. They can, however, be restored to perfection with a few swipes over a butcher's steel.

Carbon knives tarnish very easily. When working with meats this isn't a major problem. When used to cut acidic foods, however, such as onions or tomatoes, the surface of the knife will blacken and often impart an unpleasant aroma and taste to the food you are cutting.

The most expensive kitchen knives you can buy are made of high carbon steel. They marry the best features of carbon and steel knives without the drawbacks of either. They don't tarnish and their edges can be honed and restored in seconds to surgical sharpness. They are made to last a lifetime. A few extra dollars spent on quality will mean dividends in time and energy saved. Using exclusively high carbon steel knives means less time keeping the edge sharp, the tarnish and rust off and, when faced with a twenty pound mound of meat, no sore muscles from trying to hack your way through it with an imperfect knife.

Before you invest in some expensive knives, consider what type of knives you will need. A boning knife aids the meatcutter in getting all the meat possible from the bone of an animal. It is a good knife to become familiar with although some people are more comfortable with and do just as good a job with a small paring knife.

For slicing, an eight- or ten-inch chef's knife is a good choice. Its balance and shape are designed to make the job go quickly with the least amount of effort on your part.

## Butcher's Steel

One other tool that should be in every meat cutter's kitchen is the butcher's steel. Nothing more than a steel or ceramic rod with a handle, it is necessary for finely honing a blade. Manual or electric knife sharpeners grind away the blade. The steel, like a barber's strop, aligns the molecules on the very edge of the blade to create the sharpest possible cutting edge. Expect to pay about $20 for a quality steel.

Remember that a dull knife is a dangerous knife. When you *force* a dull knife to do the job it was intended to do, your hand may slip. Don't compromise the quality of your knives; keep them honed to precision; take care of them and they will reward you with a lifetime of easy and safe performance.

# Casings

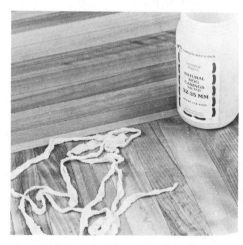

*Casings are packaged this way, and look dry and stringy when first taken from the container.*

Sausage has to be stuffed into something and that something is most often the intestine of a hog, cow, or sheep. Before you gasp, rest assured that these casings are scrupulously cleaned and are packed in salt which keeps them fresh indefinitely.

Natural casings come in an array of sizes, ranging from under one inch to a little over four inches in diameter. The smallest are usually sheep casings, ½" to 1 1/16" and the largest are from beef, 2½" to 4". Think of sheep casings as being the size of most hot dogs, and beef casings the size of a large salami. The hog casings are the most common since many sausages are made in the two-inch diameter range. Their sizes range from small (1½ inch), medium (2 inches), and large (2½ inches). All should be kept refrigerated or frozen until ready to use.

You should be familiar with two other types of casing: collagen and muslin. Collagen casings are made of natural, edible, pure protein. They generally cost a little more than intestines, are sometimes a little harder to find, but are convenient to use and usually can be substituted freely for recipes calling for natural casings.

Muslin casings can be purchased or homemade and are sometimes used with summer sausage and salami. One needn't be a Betsy Ross to stitch up a muslin casing. Just follow the instructions in Chapter 4.

Virtually every meat packing company sells hog, sheep, and beef casings and if your butcher doesn't stock them, he can order them for you. Many grocery stores, especially in ethnic neighborhoods, carry a full line of casings. These too, can be ordered by mail if you have difficulty finding them in your area. For most sausage, we recommend the natural casings.

# The Meat

In making your own sausages, be they hot dogs or salami, you get to choose not only the cut of meat but the quality as well.

The pork cuts we will be using are the butt (sometimes called the Boston butt or shoulder roast) and fresh hams. On occasion, you might find a rib or loin roast which substitutes admirably for the butt when the price is right. The loin is the leanest of the three cuts, a fact you might wish to take into consideration.

In recipes calling for beef and veal, the chuck, rump, and shank are the most economical cuts. Since most retailers sell only USDA Choice beef and veal, you can be assured of the quality.

New in this edition of *Home Sausage Making* are the chapters on making sausage from poultry and fish. We will go into more detail in those chapters about specific ingredients, but suffice it to say that chicken, turkeys, duck, goose, lobster, scallops, shrimp, and many salt water fish make for exciting sausage possibilities.

Whether you buy your sausage meat or raise and butcher your own, there is one cardinal rule which must be followed faithfully: all meat for sausage must be *very, very* fresh. The grinding process creates a proportionately greater surface area in relation to the weight of the meat. The more surface area, the bigger the breeding ground for bacteria. All meat contains bacteria, some good, some bad, some innocuous. Under optimum conditions, these bacteria are not allowed to reproduce and taint the sausage.

## Extenders

Sausage extenders include soy protein concentrate, soy flour, and powdered skim milk. There is a common misconception that these are added to sausage to "extend" the meat at a lower price. This isn't the case. Extenders are added to some sausages to make them more moist and juicy or to give them a particular texture.

# Spices and Herbs

Spices and herbs form a small part of the complete mix of a sausage, yet they in large part decide the success of the recipe.

The best of all possible worlds is to grow your own herbs and spices. This, of course, is not usually practical. Buy your spices in small quantities. If possible, store them in sealed containers in the refrigerator. If this isn't possible, at least make sure that you store them in a cool, dark place. Any spices still hanging around your pantry after a year should be deep-sixed, since their flavor most likely will more closely resemble that of sawdust than of the essence they are supposed to impart.

Although we will save our words on the use of nitrates for a later chapter, I should point out, at this point, that among the ingredients used by some in making sausage are concentrated chemicals mixed and sold as cures. Two common cures are Prague Powder #1, a general purpose sausage and meat cure containing sodium nitrate, and Prague Powder #2, a cure for dry sausages, containing sodium nitrate and sodium nitrite. Only 8 ounces of such a product is used to cure 200 pounds of meat.

# Chapter 3

# Sausage and Your Health

*F*orty-two percent of what most of us eat in any given day is composed of *fat*.

The average American consumes *three to four teaspoons of salt* a day, even though the normal adult needs only one-tenth of a teaspoon to maintain good health.

In a given year, the typical American consumes *several pounds* of the more than *3000* additives on the market that are at one time or another added to the food we eat.

Fat. Salt. Chemical additives. For more than a decade now, nutritionists and scientists have been telling us to decrease or eliminate them from our diets. True, we need some fat and salt to survive. But not dozens of times our daily minimum requirements. And additives: how many of them are really necessary and how many are there simply to make the food we eat look better, or taste fresher (even when it is not), or last longer on the shelf?

And where does sausage fit into this picture? Commercial pork sausage derives more than 75% of its calories from fat. And it also has more than its share of salt and additives. One would be hard pressed to find a single nutritionist or doctor who would recommmend that we eat such food with anything even remotely resembling regularity.

Let's take a closer look at the role of fat, salt, and additives in our diet.

# Fat

If you could separate the fat from the food you eat in an average day, you would probably be shocked to find that you were ingesting as much as *eight tablespoons.* Would you consciously sit down at the table and eat eight tablespoons of fat? I doubt it. And yet that is how much "hidden" fat you are feeding your body in one day. Just the thought of it is probably enough to make most people gag.

Before we get carried away, let's put things in perspective. Everyone does need some fat in his diet. Fats in the diet are sources of essential fatty acids, without which the body cannot make fat which is necessary for cushioning internal organs and as a thermal barrier. Vitamins A, D, E, and K are known as "fat soluble" because they need molecules of fat to transport them to the cells of the body where they are needed. But how much is enough and what kinds of fat does our body need?

The Senate Select Committee on Nutrition and Human Needs has recommended that total fat intake in the American diet should be no more than 30% of daily caloric intake. That would necessitate a 12% percent reduction in what the average American currently gets in his daily diet.

And as far as kinds of fats are concerned, the fat most deleterious to our health, saturated fat, composes about 16% percent of our daily diet. Saturated fat comes from principally animal sources, including meat, milk, milk products, eggs, and two non-animal sources, palm and coconut oils.

The other two kinds of fats found in the human diet are monounsaturated and polyunsaturated. For many years now, doctors have been advising their patients to replace the saturated fats in their diets with polyunsaturated fats. Polyunsaturated fats are found mostly in vegetable sources, nuts and fish. Several studies over the years have shown that by replacing saturated fat with polyunsaturated fat, one can lower serum (blood) cholesterol and, probably, lower ones chances of developing heart and artery disease at a premature age.

Recently a new round of studies in human nutrition has focused attention on the role of monounsaturated fat in the diet. Peanuts, peanut oil, olives, olive oil, and avocados are principal sources of monounsaturates. Up until recently, it was assumed (with very little actual evidence) that monounsaturates were "neutral" in the health game; that is, they neither contributed to nor detracted from one's health. All this has changed, however, because of recent studies on people from Mediterranean countries where the consumption of olive oil in particular is traditionally higher than elsewhere in the world. Statistical evidence seems to indicate that monounsaturated oils are actually beneficial in a way that polyunsaturates are not. Monounsaturated oil seems to increase the level of high density lipoproteins, also known as "good cholesterol," and lower the level of low density lipoproteins, or "bad cholesterol," in the blood stream. What prompted the study was the fact that people in countries where olive oil is a major constituent in the diet, heart disease rates were significantly lower than elsewhere in the world.

Ideally, the human body has no need for saturated fats. Mono and polyunsaturated fats fill the nutrition bill quite nicely, without a drastic (some would say draconian) change in diet and lifestyle that most people would not tolerate.

So the question is this: how do we optimize the percentage of beneficial fats in our diets? Quite simply, by cooking with mono and polyunsaturated fats whenever possible, and by substituting them for saturated fats whenever possible. Total elimination of saturated fat in the human diet is an unrealistic goal.

# Salt

Salt is another double-edged sword. You can't live without it, but too much could literally kill you. Close to twenty percent of the American population is known to be "sodium sensitive." This means that sodium (which is almost half of the salt molecule) tends to make blood pressure rise in individuals with this sensitivity. Although there is some evidence to indicate that heavy salt consumption in non hyper-sensitive individuals does not promote high blood pressure, an over abundance of salt in the diet does have other deleterious effects on the body. For one thing, it makes the kidneys work harder.

Salt is important in the human diet because it plays a role in how the body balances the water, minerals, and nutrients dissolved in it, and how these are regulated among the body's cells. Without a proper balance of water and dissolved salts and minerals, virtually every function in the human body would cease.

The fact of the matter is, we need only about a teaspoon of salt in our daily diet. Many common foods contain sodium. Most vegetables are naturally high in sodium. Baked goods and dairy products contain added salt for various reasons. One could literally throw the salt shaker out the window and never have a worry about getting enough salt in the diet. The problem for some people would still be too much salt.

The problem is similar to the one we encountered with fat in the diet. Without a total and radical change in diet and lifestyle, one cannot totally eliminate all the excess salt in one's diet. The solution is similar: minimize unnecessary salt untake.

# Food Additives

Of the three thousand or so food additives currently available in the food processing industry, no two have enjoyed so much publicity and notoriety as sodium and potassium nitrate and sodium nitrite. Because these chemicals are more closely related to sausage making than most of the other additives, let's take a closer look at what they are, what they do, and what can come from ingesting them.

Sodium and potassium *nitrate* (also known as saltpeter) and sodium *nitrite* are white granular chemicals that closely resemble ordinary table salt. In fact, there have been times in history where one of these chemicals was mistaken for table salt with tragic consequences.

The nitrates have been with us since the age of the Roman Empire. They have been used as curative (preservative) agents for two thousand years. Early in this century sodium nitrite was added to the preservative arsenal. Most nitrate is, in fact, converted to nitrite during the curing process.

Nitrates are naturally occuring chemicals. They are commonly found in leafy green vegetables, broccoli, and beets. Nitrites occur naturally in human saliva.

If these chemicals have been around for thousands of years, then why all of a sudden the controversy? It seems that as nitrates break down to nitrites, nitrites can also break down or aid in the formation of nitrosamines. Nitrosamines are a highly potent carcinogen. If conditions are right, then nitrosamines can form in meats which have been preserved with nitrates or nitrites.

Nitrates and nitrites are currently the most effective chemicals (if, indeed, not the only chemicals) for preventing the formation of botulism in processed meats. They also are responsible for giving cured meat its pleasing rosy color. Processed meats also owe some of their unique flavor to the chemical action of nitrates and nitrites.

The fact is, that since the publication of the first edition of this book more than five years ago, not a whole lot has changed with regard to the nitrate/nitrite question. The United States Department of Agriculture has mandated a reduction in the amount of nitrates permissible in some products. But its total elimination is not around the corner. And probably with good reason.

The question as to whether nitrates and nitrites are safe for human consumption is muddied by the fact that they are almost everywhere, including in some drinking water. No one has ever conclusively proven that they are responsible for a single human cancer. And no one has yet discovered a chemical substance that can perform their function safely.

Which brings us back to virtually the same place we were with regard to fat and salt in our diets: you can't eliminate nitrates and nitrites in your diet even if you cut out all cured meats. But you can lessen your exposure.

# Nitrates and Nitrites
# The FDA Position

Nitrates and nitrites are added to foods to prevent botulism, a form of food poisoning that is often fatal. There have been no outbreaks of botulism that were known to have been caused by foods that were treated with nitrates/nitrites. But a number of deaths have been caused by foods not treated with nitrates/nitrites. The FDA believes it is necessary for manufacturers to use these additives to prevent the growth of poisonous substances in canned ham, bacon, and in some processed meat, poultry, and fish products.

## The Risks

As with most products, nitrates and nitrites have risks as well as benefits. Under certain conditions, nitrites and amines, which are the natural breakdown products of proteins, can combine to form chemicals called nitrosamines. Experiments have shown that nitrosamines can cause cancer in animals.

There is no evidence to indicate what effects nitrosamines have in humans. We do not know, at the present time, whether the low amounts of nitrates and nitrites now permitted by regulations actually combine with amines in the stomach to form nitrosamines; nor do we know to what extent nitrosamines are formed in cured meat and fish.

The U.S. Department of Agriculture (USDA) has investigated the nitrosamine content of several products. In 48 samples of processed meats, 45 showed no nitrosamines. USDA also sampled cooked sausage which had been purchased at retail stores. Of 50 samples, 3 showed trace amounts of nitrosamines; the other 47 showed no nitrosamines.

In tests by the FDA, nitrosamines were found in one out of 60 hams tested. In another study, the FDA found that the process of cooking bacon resulted in the formation of nitrosamines in the bacon.

The levels of nitrosamines found in these samplings were extremely low—much lower than the levels that would have to be present to cause cancer in experimental animals. However, extensive study is being conducted on the entire question of how nitrates and nitrites can be used to preserve meats and yet pose no problem for human consumption.

## What is Being Done?

Based on research conducted by the meat industry in cooperation with the FDA and USDA, USDA has issued proposed regulations banning all uses of sodium nitrate in meat and poultry except in dry cured and fermented sausages, and significantly reducing the levels of nitrite allowed in other cured meats.

## In Summary

Nitrite is necessary to preserve ham, bacon, processed meats, and some smoked fish products—and thus prevent them from causing food poisoning. In regulating the use of nitrates and nitrites, the FDA must consider this benefit and weigh it against the unknown risk that these additives may help form nitrosamines which could be hazardous to health. Any change in the regulation of these additives must await the results of research now underway.

—from FDA Consumer Memo

# Where Does This Leave the Sausage Maker?

As we noted at the beginning of this chapter, the typical commercial sausage has an abundance of fat, salt, and, in some cases, chemical additives. Buy your sausage in the grocery store and you take what you get.

But there is no reason to give up sausage entirely. No one is advocating a diet composed principally of sausage. Such a diet would be just as unhealthy as one composed mostly of peanut butter and jelly on white bread.

As sausage makers, we can control to a great extent what goes into our sausage. The recipes in this book have been reformulated in many instances with an eye toward reducing the fat and salt content. Many of the fish and poultry sausages are particularly lean. The inclusion of saltpeter in the recipes for cured sausage is unequivocal since in the intervening years since the first publication of this book, the nitrate/nitrite question is no more near a solution than it was five years ago.

If you wish to avoid all added fat and salt in your diet, you will, in all probability, not be a very happy eater. Just as the human body requires some salt and fat to function properly, our taste buds require some of both because of the flavor they add and the texture they lend to food. As for nitrates and nitrites, you can't escape them. They are in the vegetables you eat, some of the water you drink, and in the saliva you swallow. If you wish to limit your exposure to them as much as possible, then you might forego eating any cured meat.

It would seem that reasonableness would indicate that, as in all things, moderation is the ultimate answer to the question about how much fat, salt, or saltpeter is too much. It would seem that we can make sausage a part of our diet and still enjoy a healthful way of eating. And having made that sausage ourselves, we can enjoy it knowing that what went into making it is not only good but good for us.

# Chapter 4

# Making Your First Batch

4 feet small (1½-inch diameter) hog or sheep casings
2½ pounds lean pork butt, cut into one inch-cubes*
½ pound pork fat, cut into one-inch cubes*
1½ teaspoons coarse salt*
¾ teaspoon finely ground white or black pepper
½ teaspoon dried thyme
1½ teaspoon dried sage
¼ teaspoon dried summer savory
¾ teaspoon sugar
½ teaspoon crushed red pepper

I n this chapter, we're going to make some country-style sausage links and I'll detail the procedures as we go along. Once you have mastered the techniques, you will be able to follow any recipe in this book with ease. Here is what you will need for three pounds of country sausage links.

## It's Next to Godliness

When making sausage you are taking on the responsibility of providing a food that is both delicious to eat and safe to eat.

Here are some rules to follow:

1. Scrub with hot water and detergent all surfaces that will be in contact with the meat. Be particularly careful of your cutting board. Rinse everything thoroughly.

2. Assemble your utensils and equipment: grinder, sausage funnel, knives, mixing spoons, and a large pan for mixing.

3. Pour boiling water over the utensils and grinder that will come into contact with the meat. Allow everything to cool completely before proceeding, so as not to raise the temperature of the meat and thus encourage the growth of bacteria.

4. Remove any rings and wash your hands carefully. Wash them again if you are called away from your work, such as for a phone call.

You're ready to begin.

---

*Note that the proportions of lean to fat as well the total amount of salt in the recipe have been reduced from the first edition of this book. The flavor remains excellent.

# Preparing the Casing

Snip off about four feet of casing. (Better too much than too little because any extra can be repacked in salt and used later.) Rinse the casing under cool running water to remove any salt clinging to it. Place it in a bowl of cool water and let it soak for about half an hour. (See illustration #1.) While you're waiting for the casing to soak, you can begin preparing the meat as detailed below.

After soaking, rinse the casing under cool running water. (See illustration #2.) Slip one end of the casing over the faucet nozzle. (See illustration #3.) Hold the casing firmly on the nozzle, and then turn on the cold water, gently at first, and then more forcefully. (See illustration #4.) This procedure will flush out any salt in the casing and pinpoint any breaks.

1

2

3

Should you find a break, simply snip out a small section of the casing. (See illustration #5.)

Place the casing in a bowl of water and add a splash of white vinegar. (See illustration #6.) A tablespoon of vinegar per cup of water is sufficient. The vinegar softens the casing a bit more and makes it more transparent, which in turn makes your sausage more pleasing to the eye. Leave the casing in the water/ vinegar solution until you are ready to use it. Rinse it well and drain before stuffing.

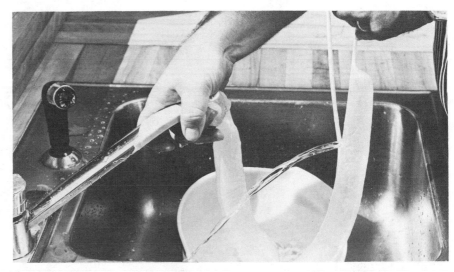

4

5

6

# Preparing the Meat

Cut the chilled pork butt into one-inch cubes, trimming off and saving the fat. (See illustration #7.) Refrigerate the meat cubes and reserved fat for about half an hour to firm them up before grinding.

If you are using a food processor, process the meat to a very fine dice and mix in the seasonings after the entire batch of meat has been processed.

If you are using a hand grinder, put the meat through the fine disk (¼" or smaller) twice. (See illustration #8.) Mix in the seasonings with your hands between the first and second grindings. (See illustration #9 and #10.)

If you are using an electric grinder with a sausage stuffing attachment, sprinkle the seasonings over the meat and mix with your hands *before* grinding since the grinding and stuffing will be one continuous operation.

7

8

9

10

# Stuffing the Sausage

Slide a piece of prepared casing over the sausage funnel or over the electric grinder's attachment. (See illustration #11.) Push it along until it is all on the funnel and the end of the casing is even with the funnel opening.

If you are using an electric stuffer, turn it on and feed the seasoned cubes of meat into the hopper. When the ground meat mixture is flush with the opening of the tube, turn off the grinder. Pull about two inches of casing off the tube and tie it into a knot. Doing it this way prevents air bubbles from getting into the sausage.

If you are using a sausage funnel, push the ground meat mixture through with your fingers until it reaches the lip of the opening and then tie off the casing. (See illustration #12.)

11

12

Continue stuffing the casing until all the meat has been used. Feed small amounts of meat through the funnel at a time, packing the casing firmly but not to the bursting point. If the casings are packed too firmly, you will be unable to twist off the links without rupturing the casing. Try to maintain an even thickness throughout the length of the casing. Try to avoid trapping air in the casing. When all the meat has been used, remove any left over casing from the funnel. (See illustration #13.)

Beginning at the tied end of the stuffed casing, grasp about three inches of sausage and give it two or three twists in the same direction to form a link. (See illustration #14.) Continue twisting off links until the entire length of casing is done. (See illustration #15.) With a very sharp knife, cut the

13

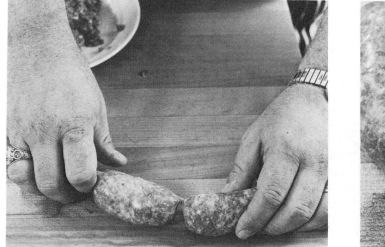

14

15

links apart and cut off any empty casing at the end. (See illustration #16.) The casing will fit the mixture like a glove and the mixture won't squeeze out. Cooking will firm up the links so the meat will not pour out even though the ends of the links are open.

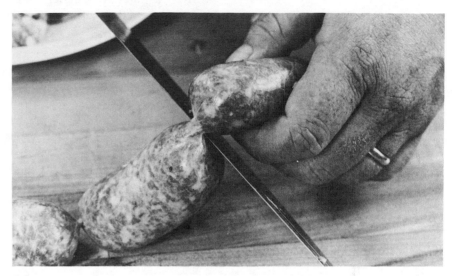

16

# Before Eating

Sausage tastes better if it ages so that the herbs and spices can penetrate the meat more completely. Arrange the links in a single layer on a platter and refrigerate them for a couple of hours.

# Cooking

Fresh sausage should be cooked slowly and thoroughly, because of the raw pork it contains. Patties can be pan fried. Sausage in casings should be simmered for five minutes and then slowly grilled until browned and cooked through.

# Storing

If you are not going to eat the sausage within two days, wrap the links individually in plastic wrap and pack them into a plastic freezer bag and freeze. Frozen sausages will hold their flavor for about three months. Thaw them completely before cooking.

# Chapter 5

# Fresh Sausage Recipes

**N**ow that you have made your first batch of homemade sausage, you are ready to try any of the recipes for fresh sausage in this chapter. The techniques for making any kind of fresh sausage are basically the same.

If your family has a favorite sausage, try that one next. You will be able to compare your results with the commercial variety and judge just how superior your homemade variety really is.

In this chapter, you will note that one thing is conspicuous in its absence: any kind of preservative. Commercially prepared fresh sausages often have preservatives added to them to extend their shelf life. Homemade sausage, on the other hand, is *made* fresh to be *eaten* fresh. If it won't be eaten in a couple of days, it should be frozen.

Before we begin, two final thoughts about the recipes in this chapter. First, the recipes here are intended to be *guides.* They are not cast in stone. Don't be afraid to experiment with them. Get a feel for the various combinations of ingredients and how they accent or contrast with one another. The next time you make the same recipe, try making small changes in the variety or amounts of the herbs and spices to suit your own tastes. Personalize the recipes and you can truly say you have made homemade sausage. By the same token, if you find yourself with a large batch of meat, feel free to double or triple the recipes. In this case, it might be prudent to cook up a small portion of a seasoned meat to taste in case the amount of seasonings needs adjustment.

Second, if you are familiar with the first edition of *Home Sausage Making*, you will notice that many of the recipes which follow have been changed slightly to reflect the desirability of a lower fat and salt content. In some cases, the amounts of other herbs and spices have also been altered. The reason for this is that when the salt (and to some extent the fat) content is lowered, people who are used to tasting highly salted food perceive low salt food as bland. One's palate must be reeducated to appreciate the taste of *un*salt. Various herbs and spices can aid in that learning process.

# German Wursts

*Wurst* means sausage, and this is a good place to start because the Germans are probably responsible for more varieties of sausage than any other group of people in the world. Here are some favorites.

## Bockwurst

*To make two pounds you will need:*

2 feet small (1½-inch diameter) hog casings
1¾ pounds veal, cubed
¼ pound pork fat, cubed
¼ cup very finely minced onion
1 cup milk
1 egg
¾ teaspoon ground cloves
½ teaspoon freshly ground white pepper
2 teaspoons finely chopped Italian (broadleaf parsley)
½ teaspoon salt, or to taste

1. Prepare the casings. (See Chapter 4.)
2. Grind the veal and pork fat separately through the fine disk of the grinder. If you are using a food processor follow the guidelines in Chapter 4.
3. Add the onion, milk, egg (well beaten), cloves pepper, parsley, and salt to the meat and mix well.
4. Put the mixture through the fine blade of the grinder.
5. Stuff mixture into the casings and twist off into three- or four-inch links. The sausage may be refrigerated for two days or so or may be boiled for thirty minutes and eaten immediately.

## Bratwurst

*Bratwurst resembles plump hot dogs. This recipe makes three pounds.*

3 feet small (1½-inch diameter) hog casings
1½ pounds lean pork butt, cubed
1 pound veal, cubed
½ pound pork fat, cubed
¼ teaspoon ground allspice
½ teaspoon crushed caraway seeds
½ teaspoon dried marjoram
1 teaspoon freshly ground white pepper
1 teaspoon salt, or to taste

1. Prepare the casings. (See Chapter 4.)
2. Grind the pork, veal, and pork fat separately through the fine blade of the grinder.
3. Mix the ground meats and grind again.
4. Add the remaining ingredients to the meat mixture and mix thoroughly.
5. Stuff the mixture into the casings and twist off into four- or five-inch lengths.
6. Refrigerate for up to two days. The bratwurst can be pan fried or grilled over charcoal.

# Frankfurter

*The lowly hot dog is the most widely consumed sausage in the world. It is also a nutritional nightmare. Fat, water, and salt make up more than fifty percent of the typical hot dog's contents by weight. In addition to being nutritionally unsound, this makes the hot dog a very expensive source of protein. When all the other ingredients are factored in, the meat in a two dollar a pound package of hot dogs is more costly than a pound of* filet mignon *at more than twice the cost.*

*This doesn't have to be the case. Try this recipe.*

**3 feet sheep or small (1½-inch diameter) hog casings**
**1 pound lean pork, cubed**
**¾ pound lean beef, cubed**
**¼ pound pork fat, cubed**
**¼ cup very finely minced onion**
**1 small clove garlic, finely chopped**
**1 teaspoon finely ground coriander**
**¼ teaspoon dried marjoram**
**¼ teaspoon ground mace**
**½ teaspoon ground mustard seed**
**1 teaspoon sweet paprika**
**1 teaspoon freshly fine ground white pepper**
**1 egg white**
**1½ teaspoons sugar**
**1 teaspoon salt, or to taste**
**¼ cup milk**

1. Prepare the casings. (See Chapter 4.)
2. In a blender or food processor, make a puree of the onion, garlic, coriander, marjoram, mace, mustard seed, and paprika.
3. Add the pepper, egg white, sugar, salt, and milk and mix thoroughly.
4. Grind the pork, beef, and fat cubes through the fine blade separately. Mix together and grind again.
5. Mix the seasonings into the meat mixture with your hands. This tends to be a sticky procedure, so wet your hands with cold water first.
6. Chill the mixture for half an hour, then put the mixture thorough the fine blade of the grinder once more.
7. Stuff the casings and twist them off into six-inch links.
8. Parboil the links (without separating them) in *gently* simmering water for twenty minutes.
9. Place the franks in a bowl of ice water and chill throughly.
10. Remove, pat dry, and refrigerate. Because they are precooked, they can be refrigerated for up to a week or they can be frozen.

# Liverwurst

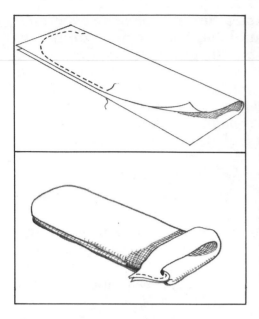

*Liverwurst is one of the most popular of all the German sausages. A thick slice sandwiched between two slices of homemade bread with a slice of Bermuda or Vidalia onion, is wickedly delicious.*

*This recipe is slightly different from the previous ones in that we don't use animal casings. You will need a piece of unbleached muslin about twelve inches long and eight inches wide. As an alternative, you can use large collagen casings.*

*Fold the muslin lengthwise and tightly stitch a seam across one of the short ends and continue along the open side. Keep the stitching about an eighth of an inch from the edge of the material. The short side of the seam can be curved in a semicircle to give the finished product a rounded end. Turn the casing inside out so that the stitching is on the inside. Set it aside until you are ready to stuff it.*

*For a two-pound liverwurst you will need the following ingredients:*

**1 pound fresh pork liver, cubed**
**¾ pound lean pork butt, cubed**
**¼ pound pork fat, cubed**
**1 large sweet white onion, about 1½ cups, finely diced**
**3 tablespoons powdered dry milk**
**1 teaspoon freshly fine ground white pepper**
**1½ teaspoons salt, or to taste**
**2 teaspoons paprika**
**1 teaspoon sugar**
**½ teaspoon marjoram**
**½ teaspoon finely ground coriander**
**¼ teaspoon mace**
**¼ teaspoon allspice**
**¼ teaspoon ground cardamom**

1. Put the cubes of liver, pork, and fat through the fine disk of the grinder separately and then mix and grind together.

2. Sprinkle the remaining ingredients over the ground meat and mix thoroughly with your hands.

3. Put the mixture through the fine blade of the grinder twice more, chilling the mixture for half an hour between grindings.

4. Pack the mixture into the muslin casing. It helps to fold the open end down over itself to get things started. This makes it easier to reach the bottom. Pack the meat as firmly as possible.

5. Stitch the open end closed or firmly secure it with a wire twist tie.

6. In a large kettle, bring enough water to a boil to cover the liverwurst by two or three inches.

7. Put the sausage in the boiling water and place a weight on it to keep it submerged. Two or three large dinner plates work just fine.

8. When the water returns to a boil, reduce the heat so that the water barely simmers.

9. Cook for three hours.

10. Drain out the hot water and replace it with an equal quantity of ice water.

11. When the liverwurst has cooled, refrigerate it overnight, and then remove the muslin casing.

12. Store the liverwurst in the refrigerator and eat it within ten days.

## Vienna Sausage

*Vienna sausages are traditionally a beef and pork combination. This recipe calls for the addition of some veal to give the sausage a mildly sweet flavor. For three pounds of sausage you will need:*

3 feet sheep or small (1½-inch diameter) hog casings
1 pound lean pork, cubed
1 pound lean beef, cubed
½ pound veal, cubed
½ pound pork fat, cubed
2 tablespoons finely minced onion
1 teaspoon sugar
½ teaspoon cayenne red pepper
1 teaspoon paprika
½ teaspoon finely ground mace
1½ teaspoon finely ground coriander
1½ teaspoons salt, or to taste
¼ cup plus one tablespoon flour
½ cup cold milk
½ cup cold water

1. Prepare the casings. (See Chapter 4.)
2. Grind the meats and fat separately through the fine disk of the grinder and mix together.
3. Mix all the remaining ingredients with the meat.
4. Put the mixture through the fine disk.
5. Stuff the casings and twist off into four-inch links. Do not separate the links.
6. Place the links in a kettle and cover with water. Bring to a boil, reduce heat, and barely simmer for forty-five minutes.
7. Remove the links, cool in cold water, pat dry, and refrigerate. Vienna sausages are excellent grilled over an open fire or they can be reheated in boiling water for ten minutes. Use within a week or freeze.

# Italian-Style Sausages

The tantalizing aroma of an Italian sausage grilling over an open fire is inspiration enough for a poet. A roasted link, wrapped in a slice of crusty homemade bread, and smothered with sautéed onions and sweet peppers, spurting juice on the first bite is sinfully delicious.

## Cotechino

*The best cut of meat to use for cotechino is a fresh ham, because part of the flavor and texture of this sausage is dependent on pork skin with which this cut of meat is usually marketed. The next time fresh hams are on sale at your local grocery, try this recipe. For six pounds:*

4—5 feet small (1½-inch diameter) hog casings

5 pounds lean fresh ham, cubed

1 pound pork skin with fat, cubed

3 teaspoons salt, or to taste

4 teaspoons coarse freshly ground black pepper

2 teaspoons ground nutmeg

2 teaspoons ground cinnamon

1 teaspoon cayenne red pepper

1 teaspoon finely ground cloves

¼ cup freshly grated Parmesan cheese

1. Prepare the casings. (See Chapter 4.)
2. Grind the meat and skin coarsely.
3. Mix the remaining ingredients with the meat and grind through the fine disk.
4. Stuff the mixture into casings and twist off into six- or eight-inch links.
5. Separate the links and allow them to dry, uncovered, in the refrigerator for two days. Turn them often so that they dry evenly.
6. You can boil them for forty-five minutes and eat them, or boil, cool, and pack into canning jars. Pour hot melted fat over them to cover, and store them in the refrigerator for up to a month. To use, scoop the sausages out of the jar and reheat them. If they are drained well after reheating, they are not nearly as high in fat as you might think.

## Luganega

*Luganega is a very mild Italian-style sausage. It is of Northern Italian origin.*

*To make four pounds of luganega you will need:*

4 feet medium (2-inch diameter) hog casings

3½ pounds lean pork butt, cubed

½ pound pork fat, cubed

1 cup freshly grated Parmesan cheese

½ teaspoon freshly grated nutmeg

½ teaspoon finely ground coriander

1 teaspoon grated lemon peel

1 teaspoon grated orange peel

1 teaspoon freshly fine ground black pepper

1 small clove garlic, very finely chopped

1½ teaspoons salt, or to taste

½ cup dry vermouth

1. Prepare the casings. (See Chapter 4.)
2. Grind the pork and fat together through the fine disk.
3. Sprinkle the remaining ingredients over the meat and mix well.
4. Stuff the mixture into casings and twist off into eight- or ten-inch lengths.
5. Separate the links and allow them to dry in a cool place for two or three hours.
6. Refrigerate and use within two or three days or freeze. The flavor of the lemon and orange is intensified by freezing so the sausage is best used fresh.

## Northern Italian-Style Hot or Sweet Sausage

*This variety is easy to make and is delicious roasted or used to flavor tomato sauce. To make three pounds:*

3 feet medium (2-inch diameter) hog casings
2½ pounds lean pork butt, cubed
½ pound pork fat, cubed
1½ teaspoons salt, or to taste
2 teaspoons freshly coarse ground black pepper
2 teaspoons finely ground coriander
2 cloves garlic, finely minced
1 teaspoon crushed red pepper for hot sausage, or to taste

1. Prepare the casings. (See Chapter 4.)
2. Grind the meat and fat together through the coarse disk.
3. Mix the remaining ingredients together with the meat.
4. Stuff into the casings and twist off into three-inch links.
5. Refrigerate and use within three days or freeze.

## Sicilian-Style Hot or Sweet Sausage

*Choose which version you will make and then:*

*Ingredients for version #1:*

5 feet medium (2-inch diameter) hog casings
4½ pounds lean pork butt, cubed
½ pound pork fat, cubed
2½ teaspoons salt, or to taste
3 teaspoons freshly coarse ground black pepper
3 teaspoons fennel seed
Crushed red pepper to taste for hot sausage

*Ingredients for version #2:*

Same as above except add:
2 cloves garlic, finely minced
1 teaspoon anise seed

1. Prepare the casings. (See Chapter 4.)
2. Grind the meat and fat together through the coarse disk.
3. Mix the remaining ingredients together with the meat and fat.
4. Stuff the mixture into casings and twist off into three- or four-inch links.
5. Refrigerate and use within three days or freeze.

# Other Fresh Sausages

## Lamb Sausage with Rosemary

*One doesn't ordinarily associate lamb with sausage, but the delicate flavor of true spring lamb can make a delicious sausage.*

4 feet sheep or small (1½-inch diameter) hog casings

2½ pounds lean spring lamb, cubed

½ pound lamb or pork fat, cubed

1 teaspoon freshly coarse ground black pepper

1 tablespoon fresh or 1½ teaspoons dried rosemary

1 clove garlic, finely minced

1 teaspoon salt, or to taste

1. Prepare the casings. (See Chapter 4.)
2. Mix the meat and fat cubes with the seasonings.
3. Grind the mixture through the fine blade of the grinder.
4. Stuff the mixture into the casings and twist off into three-inch links.
5. Refrigerate and use within three days or freeze.

## Lamb Sausage with Mint

*For three pounds:*

4 feet sheep or small (1½-inch diameter) hog casings

2½ pounds lean spring lamb, cubed

½ pound lamb or pork fat, cubed

1 teaspoon freshly coarse ground black pepper

2 tablespoons fresh or 2 teaspoons dried mint leaves (for a variation use lemon, pineapple, apple or other mint instead of the usual spear or peppermint)

¼ teaspoon grated lemon zest

1 teaspoon salt, or to taste

1. Prepare the casings. (See Chapter 4.)
2. Mix the meat and fat cubes with the seasonings.
3. Grind the mixture through the fine blade of the grinder.
4. Stuff the mixture into the casings and twist off into three-inch links.
5. Refrigerate and use within three days or freeze.

# Boudin Blanc

Boudin blanc *is French for "white pudding," which doesn't justly describe these mild and finely textured little sausages. Here's what you will need for about three pounds:*

4 feet medium (2-inch diameter) hog casings
½ pound pork fat, cubed
1 cup milk
¾ cup dry bread crumbs
1 pound veal, cubed
1 pound boneless, skinless, breast of chicken
3 large onions, peeled and sliced
¼ teaspoon nutmeg
¼ teaspoon allspice
¼ teaspoon finely ground fresh white pepper
1 teaspoon salt, or to taste
1 tablespoon chopped parsley
1 tablespoon chopped chives
2 eggs
2 egg whites
1 cup heavy cream

1. Prepare the casings. (See Chapter 4.)

2. Grind the pork fat through the fine disk.

3. Place *half* the ground fat in the skillet and melt it down slowly over medium heat.

4. Add the onions to the rendered fat and cook slowly in a covered skillet for fifteen to twenty minutes or until the onions are translucent.

5. In another pan, bring the milk to a boil and add the bread crumbs. Cook, stirring constantly, until the mixture thickens enough to stick to the spoon when the spoon is inverted.

6. Grind the veal and chicken together through the fine disk.

7. Combine and mix thoroughly the onions, remaining fat, veal and chicken, nutmeg, allspice, pepper, salt, parsley, and chives. Grind the mixture through the fine disk.

8. In a food processor or with an electric mixer, blend the mixture until it is thoroughly mixed. Continue beating or mixing and add the eggs and egg whites. Beat a couple of minutes more and then add the bread crumbs.

9. Continue beating and add the cream, a little at a time.

10. Stuff the mixture into the casings and twist off into four-inch links. Refrigerate, covered, for one or two days.

11. Prick the casings with a needle and place them in a large pot. Cover them with a mixture of half milk and half water. Bring the liquid to a simmer and cook gently for thirty minutes.

12. Cool and refrigerate for up to three days. Cook by grilling or frying until just heated through.

## Chorizo

*In Spain and Mexico, you can find chorizos both fresh and dried. Either way, they are sure to satisfy one's craving for something spicy. To make four pounds of chorizos:*

5 feet medium (2-inch diameter) hog casings
3½ pounds lean pork butt, cubed
½ pound pork fat, cubed
2 teaspoons salt, or to taste
2 teaspoons freshly coarse ground black pepper
1 teaspoon crushed red pepper
4 cloves garlic, finely chopped
3 teaspoons red wine vinegar
¼ cup dry red wine
2 tablespoons brandy
1 teaspoon fennel seed

1. Prepare the casings. (See Chapter 4.)
2. Grind the meat and fat together through the coarse disk.
3. Mix the remaining ingredients together with the meat.
4. Place the mixture in a large covered pan in the refrigerator for three or four hours. This gives the wine and brandy a chance to extract the flavor from the herbs and spices and for the meat to absorb some of the liquid.
5. Stuff the mixture into the casings.
6. Refrigerate and use within three days or freeze.

## Fresh Polish Kielbasa

*Recipes for this sausage are so variable that what passes for kielbasa in one area might be regarded as not authentic in another. The ingredients and pronunciation of kielbasa are as variable as are the vagaries of the spring weather, the time of year when kielbasa is traditionally made. This version uses pork, beef, and veal and makes five pounds.*

6 feet large (2½-inch diameter) hog casings
3 pounds lean pork butt, cubed
1 pound lean beef chuck, cubed
½ pound veal, cubed
½ pound pork fat, cubed
2½ teaspoons salt, or to taste
3 teaspoons finely ground black pepper
2 teaspoons ground marjoram
2 teaspoons ground summer savory
½ teaspoon ground allspice
3 cloves garlic, finely minced
2 tablespoons sweet paprika

1. Prepare the casings. (See Chapter 4.)
2. Grind the meats and fat together through the coarse disk.
3. Mix the remaining ingredients with the meat.
4. Stuff the casings and leave the sausage in long links. Lengths of eighteen inches to two feet are traditional.
5. Allow the sausage to dry in a cool place for three or four hours or refrigerate for twenty-four hours uncovered.
6. Cook by roasting in a 425° F oven for forty-five minutes. These sausages are also excellent grilled over a charcoal fire and eaten in a Kaiser roll, lathered with a spicy brown mustard.

# Fresh Garlic Sausage

*You might think that, judging from its name, this sausage has enough garlic in it to protect you from the plague (which it probably will do) and to keep your neighbors at a respectable distance. The garlic in this recipe merely perfumes the meat. In fact, when garlic is cooked it loses much of its pungency. To make four pounds of sausage:*

**5 feet medium (2-inch diameter) hog casings**
**3½ pounds lean pork butt, cubed**
**½ pound pork fat, cubed**
**2 teaspoons sugar**
**4 teaspoons garlic, finely minced**
**1 teaspoon finely ground black pepper**
**1 tablespoon salt, or to taste**
**¼ teaspoon freshly grated nutmeg**
**¼ teaspoon freshly grated cinnamon**
**1 teaspoon fresh finely chopped ginger**
**¼ teaspoon ground allspice**
**¼ teaspoon ground thyme**
**½ cup dry white wine or dry vermouth**

1. Prepare the casings. (See Chapter 4.)
2. Grind the meat and fat together through the fine disk.
3. Mix the ground meat with all the remaining ingredients. Combine thoroughly.
4. Stuff the casings and twist off into four-inch links.
5. Dry, uncovered, in the refrigerator for a day or two, turning them often.
6. Cook by boiling in water or chicken stock or freeze.

# Potatis Korv

## (Swedish Potato Sausage)

*This sausage is very popular in Sweden. For about five pounds of sausage:*

**4 feet medium (2-inch diameter) hog casings**
**1 pound very lean beef, cubed**
**½ pound lean pork butt, cubed**
**½ pound pork fat, cubed**
**5 large potatoes**
**1 large onion, peeled and chopped coarsely**
**½ teaspoon freshly ground white pepper**
**½ teaspoon freshly ground black pepper**
**2 teaspoons salt, or to taste**
**¼ teaspoon ground allspice**
**¼ teaspoon ground nutmeg**
**1 clove garlic, very finely minced**
**¼ teaspoon ground mace**
**Chicken broth**

1. Prepare the casings. (See Chapter 4.)

2. Grind the meats and fat separately through the fine disk. Refrigerate until you are ready for step five.

3. Peel and boil the potatoes in lightly salted water for ten minutes. They should be quite firm in the center. Allow them to cool before proceeding to the next step.

4. Cube the potatoes and mix together with the chopped onion. Put this mixture through the fine disk of the grinder.

5. Add the ground meats to the potatoes and onion. Add all remaining ingredients and mix well. The mixture will be quite sticky, so it will help if you run cold water over your hands and leave them wet for the mixing.

6. Stuff the mixture into the casings.

7. Twist off into twelve-inch links. With cotton butcher's twine, tie two separate knots between each link and one knot at each end. Separate the links by cutting between the two knots between each pair of links. Bring the ends of each link together and tie to form rings.

8. Boil the rings in well seasoned chicken broth for forty-five minutes. The sausages may be eaten warm or refrigerated and served cool.

# Preserving Sausage

Long before refrigeration, there was the need for long term preservation of meat. Our ancestors faced either feast or famine. When someone made a kill everyone feasted. Sometimes, probably more often than not, feasts were far between. Man's ingenuity eventually led him to discover new ways in which foodstuffs could be preserved between kills, and could be easily transported and consumed when needed.

Drying is probably the oldest method of food preservation known to man. He learned that most of the bacteria that cause food to spoil cannot survive without water.

This is good news for the home sausage maker.

Homemakers in antiquity may not have known *why* drying worked, but they knew that it *did* work. Alexis Soyer, in his 1853 history of food, *The Pantropheon*, describes a recipe for an Italian sausage he calls "Lucanian sausage." After instructing the cook in the proper technique of adding the various ingredients such as garum, gravy, bacon, and pine nuts, he tells the maker to hang up the sausage to dry. Since the recipe is traced by Soyer back to the Roman poet, Virgil, we can rest assured that the method has stood the test of time.[1]

# What is Spoilage?

Any dictionary will tell you that "to spoil" means "to become rotten, decayed or otherwise unfit for use as food." That's fine as far as it goes, but it doesn't explain the process.

Spoilage is caused by the action of microorganisms on foodstuffs. Microorganisms can be divided into three groups: molds, yeasts, and bacteria.

---

[1]Alexis Soyer, *The Pantropheon: or A History of Food and its Preparation in Ancient Times*, reprint of 1853, ed., New York, 1977, p. 141.

Molds, such as the blue-green growth you find on stale bread, can harm our cured sausage (and us in turn). Some molds are capable of producing a substance called mycotoxin which can make people extremely ill.

Yeasts are probably the least dangerous of all microorganisms. This isn't to say that they are necessarily welcome guests. Yeasts can be good things; they are responsible for bread rising and grape juice turning into alcohol.

Bacteria are the most troublesome microorganisms with which the sausage maker has to deal. They are everywhere. But like many things in life, the bacteria problem is a double-edged sword. Without them, life could not exist as we know it. Yet, if some types of bacteria were allowed to reproduce in an uncontrolled environment, human life would cease to exist.

Anyone working with food must be alert to the four most common causes of bacterial food poisoning: *Salmonella*, *Clostridium perfringens*, *Staphylococcus*, and *Clostridium botulinum.*

All four are found throughout our environment and in most foods. All can cause illness and even death.

*Salmonella* is the most common source of food poisoning in man. These bacteria can survive in frozen and dried foods, but do not reproduce at temperatures below 40° F or above 140° F, and they are destroyed if food is held above 140° F for ten minutes.

*Clostridium perfringens* can also strike if food is held at improper temperatures for an extended period of time.

Both this bacterium and *Staphylococcus aureus* are inactive at temperatures below 40° F and above 140° F. If staph germs are allowed to multiply, they form a toxin that cannot be boiled or baked away.

*Clostridium botulinum* organisms are the biggest villains in the microorganism arsenal. They love room temperature and moisture, and are anaerobic, which means that they thrive and produce toxin in an environment that lacks oxygen. Given the proper conditions, they produce spores so resilient that they would make any science fiction writer thrilled to have thought of them before Mother Nature. These spores are harmless, but when they reproduce, they give off a toxin that is so deadly that about two cups of it could kill every human being in a city the size of New York. The toxin can be killed by ten to twenty minutes of boiling, but the spores require six hours of boiling to render them inactive.

Fortunately, we can prevent these bacteria from setting up shop in our homemade sausage.

# Preventing Spoilage

As anyone who has ever put up canned foodstuffs can tell you, an ounce of prevention is worth a pound of cure.

When we were getting ready to make fresh sausage, we mentioned that cleanliness is an absolute priority in sausage making. If we keep in mind the following rules, we can keep the problem of food spoilage to an absolute minimum:

**Rule 1:** Sterilize all utensils that come in contact with the sausage as it is being prepared.

**Rule 2:** Keep your work area clear, uncluttered, and scrupulously clean. This is a safety rule as well as a sanitation rule.

**Rule 3:** Wash your hands thoroughly and often. Bacteria absolutely *thrive* at body temperature.

**Rule 4:** Keep meat cool at all times. Work quickly and refrigerate meats as soon as possible.

These rules make a lot more sense if you know what prevents bacterial growth. Inhibiting factors include:

- Temperatures below 40° F or above 140° F

- An acid or sugary environment

- A lack of moisture

- Salt

- Alcohol (to some extent)

- Some chemical additives

The more we tailor our sausage's environment to take into account these factors, the more certain we can be of its safety and purity.

# What About Nitrates and Nitrites?

Refer to Chapter 3 for a detailed discussion of sodium and potassium nitrate and sodium nitrite. But in considering whether or not to make cured sausages containing these preservatives, consider these possibilities:

1. Make cured sausages using the recipes that follow and include saltpeter (a nitrate) or substitute one of the commercially available cures, such as Morton's *Tender Quick* or *Prague Powder #1* or *#2*, following the directions that come with the package.

2. Make these same sausages, but include Vitamin C as an ingredient since it has been shown that this chemical prevents some of the nitrosamine formation which has given nitrates a bad name.

3. Confine your making of sausage to fresh varieties. Further, when reducing the amount of salt in a recipe, if you are unsure or in doubt about the storage possibilities of a particular sausage, treat it as fresh sausage.

One final note about Vitamin C: be sure to purchase pure crystalline ascorbic acid from your pharmacist and make sure that the label states that it is "U.S.P." This means that it is intended for human consumption.

# The Trichinosis Problem

Several cases of trichinosis are reported in the United States every year. The number of cases each year is declining, but the possibility of trichinosis contamination is still a real possibility.

Trichinosis is a disease caused by a parasitic roundworm, *Trichinella spiralis*, or, in English, trichina. The worm, found in some pork and bear meat, can be transmitted to humans if the meat is eaten raw or untreated.

Trichinae mature in a person's intestines and are usually killed by the body's defenses. Some, however, can survive in the form of cysts in various muscles for years.

Trichinosis, however, need not be a problem for the home sausage maker. In the case of fresh pork not used for sausage, the meat need only be cooked to an internal temperature of 137° F. Pork to be consumed raw, as in dried sausage, can be made completely safe and free of trichinae by freezing it to −20° F for six to twelve days, −10° F for ten to twenty days or 5° F for twenty to thirty days. An accurate freezer thermometer is a must if you intend to prepare pork for dried sausage. These guidelines have been set by the USDA for commercial packers and are perfectly safe if followed by the home sausage maker. Never taste raw pork and never sample sausage if it contains raw pork that hasn't been treated as we have described.

If for some reason you can't or don't wish to tie up freezer space to treat your own sausage meat, you can ask your butcher to order you some "certified" pork. Certified pork has been frozen to render it trichinosis free and comes stamped or labeled as such. Make sure that you see the stamp or label.

# Drying Equipment

## The Attic:

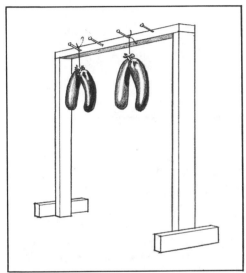

If you have all the equipment necessary to make fresh sausage, you need one more thing to make dried sausage—a cold place to dry your sausage and let it hang for a few weeks. (You might also want to invest in a smoker, but we'll get to that a bit later). Choose a place that is convenient and not needed for other purposes while the sausage is drying. Here are a few suggestions.

People who live in northern climates traditionally make their dried sausages in the winter. If you use your attic, make sure of the following:

1. The temperature must remain below 40° F for the drying time indicated in the recipes. The temperature in the attic shouldn't fall *below* freezing for extended periods of time either. You don't want to freeze the sausage, you want to dry it.

2. Be certain that no birds or rodents can find their way into the attic. It would be very disconcerting to find a squirrel, or something else, swinging from your salami.

3. The attic should be clean. Sweep away dust and dirt several days before you plan to hang sausage. What the broom doesn't pick up will have a chance to settle before the sausage is hung.

4. Pound four-inch nails, spaced twelves inches apart, half way into a rafter for hanging the sausage. If the rafters are covered, a simple frame can be constructed from 2' × 4''s.

Attics are a particularly good place to dry sausage if they have vents to provide cross ventilation and thus speed the drying process.

# The Refrigerator:

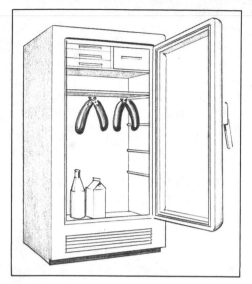

Use the refrigerator in your kitchen only as a last resort. You will be tying up the space for a long period of time and it may prove very inconvenient to have to dodge the drying salami each time you want to get out a quart of milk.

If you have a second refrigerator or can obtain one cheaply, using it can be as practical as the attic. If you live in a warm climate, this should be your first choice.

Remove all the shelves except the top one. The sausages can be tied to hang from this shelf.

If you choose to use a refrigerator, use a thermometer to make sure that the temperature remains constantly in the 38–40° F range. If the refrigerator has a fan, and most modern ones do, it must be adjusted so as not to blow constantly. Too much air movement would cause the sausage to dry on the outside before the inside had a chance to mature.

# Other Solutions

Use your imagination. An unheated part of the house is a possibility. An unheated cellar might work also, but in either case, be sure to provide enough ventilation.

If none of these methods work for you, investigate renting space in a local meat locker plant. Most such plants have cooling rooms used for aging meat that are kept at a constant temperature.

# How the Drying Process Works

In the recipes in the next chapter, you will be relying on basically three things to preserve your sausage: salt (and saltpeter or a commercial cure), alcohol, and temperature.

Alcohol begins the preservation process. In addition to being an excellent flavor enhancer, it has known antibacterial properties. The alcohol evaporates, however, and so we need other agents to continue the work.

Salt and saltpeter get into the act long before the alcohol is gone. Salt draws the moisture out of the meat. Molds and bacteria have a difficult time when moisture is lacking.

Temperature is almost as important as salt. Those nasty little creatures that cause spoilage don't like low temperatures.

# A Word About Ingredients

Everything said in the first chapter about ingredients used in sausage applies here. And here is a word of caution: the drying process intensifies and concentrates flavors. This gives dried sausages their "spicy" reputation. Use only the purest and freshest herbs and spices.

The recipes in the next chapter call for varying amounts of alcohol. While it would be wasteful to use expensive wines and brandies from vintage years, the cheapest jug wines or bargain basement brandy are also poor choices. The cardinal rule in using alcohol in food is, "If you wouldn't drink it, don't cook with it."

All wines and spirits contain substances known as "congeners." These substances are responsible for giving the alcohol its characteristic flavor. Cheaper wines and spirits contain "rougher" versions of these agents and, when concentrated in a dried sausage, can lend it some off flavors.

# Smoking

*An electric home smoker like this will smoke up to forty pounds of meat at one time. Door has been removed to show interior.*

Smoking cured pork sausage improves its appearance and gives it a characteristic flavor and aroma. Careful attention must be given to prevent spoilage.

Smoking is an art, the basics of which can be taught. Like any other art, practice makes perfect, and one has to learn the "feel" of the method to turn out a consistantly good product.

The USDA has set forth in understandable terms the principles and procedures for smoking. The following discussion is based closely on its guidelines.

## Guidelines for Smoking Sausages

1. Smoke only meat that is dry on the surface. A wet surface prevents meat from gaining a uniform smoked color.

2. Hang sausages so that they do not touch each other or the smokehouse wall. The entire surface of the meat must be exposed to ensure an even color.

3. For a fire, use a hardwood such as hickory, oak, apple, cherry, pear, beech, chestnut, pecan or maple. Mesquite, a hardwood shrub from the Southwest, provides a unique aroma which has become very popular of late. Dry corncobs can also be used. Never use softwoods such as pine, cedar, spruce, hemlock, fir or cypress. They give off a sooty smoke which give your sausage a dark, bitter taste.

# Smoke-houses:

The smokehouse can be simple or elaborate in design depending upon the quantity of meat to be smoked. If you are simply a "weekend smoker", then a small portable gas or electric smoker is sufficient. There are several on the market.

If you have the need, time, and initiative (and space) you might want to construct a permanent smokehouse. Your structure should be of reasonably tight construction and permit easy regulation of temperature and flow of air. Be sure to check local building and fire codes.

Temporary smokehouses can be constructed easily and cheaply. Construction should include a ventilated enclosure for hanging and smoking sausage as well as facilities for generating smoke and supplying it to the house. A barrel or drum with both ends removed, connected by a stovepipe or a covered trench to a fire pit can be used. Set the barrel over the upper end of the ten to twelve foot stovepipe which slopes downward toward the fire pit. Control the heat by covering the pit with sheet metal and mounding earth around the edges to cut off the draft. Clean muslin or burlap hung over the cleated top of the barrel will protect a one-inch opening between the barrel and the cleated top that rests on the broomsticks supporting the meat. You will need a thermometer that can be mounted to extend through a hole bored in the barrel, or it can be hung from the broomsticks.

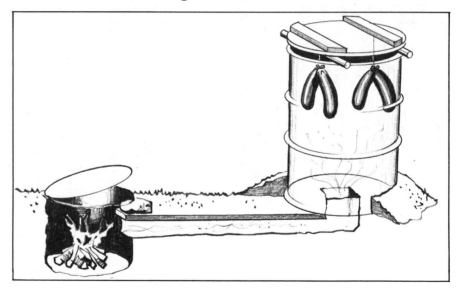

# Hot and Cold Smoking

The smoking process is either a "cold smoke" or a "hot smoke." Smoking at temperatures above 120° F is called hot smoking and cooks the meat in the process. Smoking at temperatures below 120° F is called cold smoking and is basically a flavoring process. Meat that is cold smoked is essentially raw (unless it was precooked or preserved in some other manner) and must be treated as such.

You will note that some of the recipes call for both cold and hot smoking. The cold smoking is for flavor, and the hot smoking is to cook the sausage.

# Chapter 7

# Making Cured Sausages

One of my favorite pastimes is prowling around in small ethnic grocery stores—"mom and pop" stores as they are sometimes called—because many of these places preserve the old-country tradition of making or preparing much of what they sell. One such store in my neighborhood is a favorite of mine. Walk in on a Thursday afternoon and you will find the proprietor mixing up a batch of Italian sausage for the weekend trade. Hanging from a wire stretched above the meatcase are dozens of links of salami and pepperoni along with balls of aged provolone cheese. Lining one of the walls are barrels of oil-cured olives and baskets of dried codfish—*baccala*—and brown paper bags of homemade pasta. The aromas in that little store are enough to bring on Herculean hunger pangs. The proprietor won't part with his secret recipes but he takes pride in making his sausages in full view of anyone present. It is comforting to know that not all sausage today comes packaged in plastic, having issued forth from polished chrome and stainless steel machines. Some of the best things in life are still made by hand.

# Procedures and Equipment

To make the job easier follow these procedures before making any cured sausages:

1. Prepare the work area.

2. Assemble all equipment: grinder, sausage funnel, knives, mixing spoons, and a large pan for mixing.

3. Sterilize all equipment that will come in contact with the raw sausage by pouring boiling water over it.

4. Clear a space in the refrigerator large enough to accommodate the mixing pan for overnight curing.

5. Make sure the drying area is clean and ready.

6. If the recipe calls for smoking have the smokehouse or electric smoker ready. Make sure you have enough fuel on hand because once you start smoking you don't want to have to scrounge up more wood chips.

# Salami

Of all the various kinds of dried sausages, more are probably labeled "salami" than anything else. The term salami encompasses many different sizes and shapes of highly spiced dried sausages. Some salami are short and fat, some are quite long. Some have a distinct smoky flavor while in some, wine is the dominant flavor.

The term salami is the plural form of the Italian word *salame* which derives from the Latin word *sal*, meaning salt. The sausage gets its name from the ingredient that gives it some of its flavor and helps preserve it. Whether you prefer it sliced thin and piled high in a submarine sandwich or cubed and sautéed with onions as a base for a rich tomato sauce, you will have to admit that the culinary world is a much more exciting place, thanks to salami.

Here are several recipes, at least one of which is sure to become your favorite.

## Genoa Salami

*This salami is large and robust and full of brandy. To make ten pounds you will need the following ingredients:*

5 pounds lean beef from chuck, round or shank

3 pounds lean pork butt, certified or pre-frozen, cubed*

2 pounds pork fat, cubed*

5 tablespoons salt

1 cup good quality brandy

1½ tablespoons sugar

2 tablespoons whole peppercorns

1 tablespoon finely ground white pepper

1 teaspoon finely ground coriander seed

2 teaspoons garlic, finely minced

1 teaspoon cardamom

½ teaspoon ascorbic acid

1 teaspoon saltpeter

4 feet large (3½—4-inch diameter) beef casings

1. Grind the beef, pork, and fat separately through the coarse disk.

2. Mix the beef, pork, and fat together and chill in the freezer for about thirty minutes.

3. Grind the mixture through the fine disk.

4. Mix the remaining ingredients with the meat.

5. Cure the mixture in the refrigerator for twenty-four hours.

6. Prepare the casings. (See Chapter 4.)

7. Pack the mixture into the casings and tie off into twelve-inch links, and hang them to dry. Since the salami is very thick sausage, eight weeks is the minimum time you should allow to dry before sampling. Depending upon your specific drying conditions, twelve weeks is about the optimum drying time.

*Prepare pork according to the instructions in Chapter 6 to assure that it is trichinosis free.

# Mild Salami

*This salami uses equal parts of beef and pork and has a milder flavor than the preceeding recipe. The recipe is for ten pounds.*

4 pounds lean beef, cubed
4 pounds lean, pre-frozen or certified pork, cubed*
2 pounds pork fat, cubed*
5 tablespoons salt
½ cup brandy
½ cup dry white wine
2 tablespoons coarse ground black pepper
1 tablespoon finely ground white pepper
1 teaspoon cayenne pepper
1 tablespoon sugar
1 teaspoon garlic, finely minced
1 teaspoon finely ground nutmeg
1 teaspoon finely ground coriander seed
1 teaspoon finely ground fennel seed
½ teaspoon ascorbic acid
1 teaspoon saltpeter
4 feet large (3½—4-inch diameter) beef casings

1. Grind the beef, pork and fat separately through the coarse disk.

2. Mix the meat and fat together and spread the mixture out on a large pan and chill in the freezer for thirty minutes.

3. Grind the meat through the fine disk.

4. Mix in the remaining ingredients.

5. Cure the mixture in the refrigerator for twenty-four hours.

6. Prepare the casings. (See Chapter 4.)

7. Pack the mixture into casings and tie off into twelve-inch links. Dry for eight to twelve weeks.

---

*Prepare pork according to the instructions in Chapter 6 to assure that it is trichinosis free.

## Soppresatta Salami

*For ten pounds of sausage you will need:*

3 pounds lean beef
5 pounds pre-frozen or certified pork*
2 pounds pork fat*
5 tablespoons salt
1 tablespoon finely ground black pepper
2 teaspoons finely ground white pepper
1 teaspoon finely ground coriander
1 teaspoon garlic, finely minced
2 teaspoons sugar
1 cup dry white wine
½ teaspoon ascorbic acid
1 teaspoon saltpeter
4 feet large (3½—4-inch diameter) beef casings

1. Grind the beef, pork and fat separately through the coarse disk and then mix together in a large pan.
2. Put all the remaining ingredients except the wine, garlic and casings into the bowl of a blender or food processor and process until you have a fine powder.
3. Add the powdered ingredients, wine, and garlic to the meat mixture and mix through well.
4. Cure in the refrigerator for twenty-four hours.
5. Prepare the casings. (See Chapter 4.)
6. Stuff the mixture into the casings and tie off into six- or seven-inch links to give the soppresatta its traditional short, stubby shape.
7. Hang the sausage to dry for eight to twelve weeks.

## Veal Salami

*This salami is different from the preceding ones in that it includes pork and veal. Even though it is still spicy enough to deserve the name salami it is sweeter than most other sausages of this type. To make ten pounds you will need:*

5 pounds lean veal cubes
3 pounds certified or pre-frozen pork, cubed*
2 pounds cubed pork fat*
5 tablespoons salt
2 tablespoons sugar
1 tablespoon finely ground black pepper
1 tablespoon finely ground white pepper
½ teaspoon nutmeg
1 teaspoon crushed anise seed
½ cup dry vermouth
½ cup brandy
½ teaspoon ascorbic acid
1 teaspoon saltpeter
4 feet large (3½—4 inch diameter) beef casings

1. Grind the veal, pork, and fat through the coarse disk separately.
2. Mix the veal and fat and put the mixture through the fine disk. It will help if the meat and fat are chilled before the grinding.
3. Mix the veal/fat mixture with the pork.
4. Mix the remaining ingredients with the meat.
5. Cure in the refrigerator for twenty-four hours.
6. Prepare the casings. (See Chapter 4.)
7. Stuff the mixture into the casings and tie off into six- or seven-inch links.
8. Hang the salami to dry for eight to twelve weeks.

*Prepare pork according to the instructions in Chapter 6 to assure that it is trichinosis free.

# Kosher Salami

*This recipe makes real kosher salami if you have access to kosher-butchered beef. If not, then just like kosher dill pickles, it's the flavor that counts. Since this is an all beef recipe, use blade cut chuck which has about the right proportions of lean to fat. Trim away all fat when cubing the meat, and, thus, precisely measure the amounts. Before you jump into this recipe, check on the smokehouse or dig out the instructions to the electric smoker because you will be needing it soon. Here is what you will need for ten pounds:*

8 pounds lean, boneless beef chuck, cubed

2 pounds beef fat, cubed

5 tablespoons salt

1½ teaspoons garlic, finely minced

1 tablespoon finely ground white pepper

1½ teaspoons coarsely crushed white pepper

1 tablespoon coarsely ground coriander seed

1½ tablespoons sugar

1 cup dry white wine

½ teaspoon ascorbic acid

1 teaspoon saltpeter

4 feet large (3½–4-inch diameter) beef casings

1. Grind the beef through the fine disk.

2. Grind the fat through the coarse disk.

3. Mix the dry ingredients with the wine and pour this mixture over the meat and fat. Mix well.

4. Spread the mixture in a large pan and cure in the refrigerator for twenty-four to forty-eight hours.

5. Prepare the casings. (See Chapter 4.)

6. Stuff the mixture into the casings and tie off into eight- or nine-inch links.

7. Hang the sausage to dry for one week.

8. Wipe the sausage dry and smoke over a cool (about 120° F) smoke for eight hours.

9. Increase the smoking temperature to 150–160° F and smoke for an additional four hours.

10. Because the smoking aids in the drying process, the salami should be ready to eat after about three weeks of additional drying.

## Beer Salami

*This salami is called "beer salami" because it is irresistible with a stein of cold lager. We're going to add a new twist to your sausage making repertoire because this sausage uses cured instead of fresh meat. It, too, requires smoking. You could cure your own pork, and corn your own brisket, or pick up some ham and corned beef at the meat counter. For ten pounds:*

3 pounds corned beef brisket, cubed

7 pounds ham, fat included, cubed*

1½ tablespoons coarsely ground black pepper

1 tablespoon ground mace

1½ tablespoons crushed mustard seed

2 teaspoons garlic, finely minced

4 feet large (3½—4-inch diameter) beef casings

1. Grind the corned beef brisket through the fine disk.

2. Mix the beef with the ham cubes and mix in the seasonings.

3. Grind the mixture thorugh the coarse disk.

4. Prepare the casings. (See Chapter 4.)

5. Stuff the mixture into the casings and tie off at six- or eight-inch intervals.

6. Store in the refrigerator for about twenty-four hours to mature.

7. Bring the salami to room temperature. This should take two to three hours. Wipe it dry.

8. Begin smoking the salami at about 80° F and *gradually* raise the smokehouse temperature to 160° F. This should take about four hours. Smoke an additional two hours.

9. Cool off the sausage by dunking it in a large pot of cool (not cold) water. Four or five minutes, or until it is cool to the touch, is sufficient.

10. Dry the salami thoroughly and store it in the refrigerator.

**Note:** Because we used cured meat in this recipe, there was no need for any other curing agents or additional salt.

---

*Prepare pork according to the instructions in Chapter 6 to assure that it is trichinosis free.

# Calabrese Salami

*This sausage is called* calabrese *in Italian because that is where it originated. The sausage is as stark as the landscape of its birthplace. Calabria is a section of Italy which time has almost passed by. The Appenines are the central geographic feature and they dictate the manner of living in the region. Although there is some tillable land, and it does produce excellent vegetables, this region is most famous for its porkers. If there is any one region of Italy that is more proud of its sausages than any other, it has to be Calabria. You no doubt would get an argument about that statement from a Sicilian.*

*If there is anything that rivals the importance of pork in Calabria, it is the fiery red peppers that this region seems so well suited to produce. Pork and lots of red pepper, that's Calabrese salami. For ten pounds:*

7 pounds lean, cubed, pre-frozen or certified pork*
3 pounds diced pork fat*
5 tablespoons salt
2 teaspoons pure anise extract flavoring (or ¼ cup anisette)
1 tablespoon finely ground white pepper
3 tablespoons crushed red hot pepper
½ cup dry vermouth
½ cup brandy
½ teaspoon ascorbic acid
1 teaspoon saltpeter
6 feet medium (2-inch diameter) hog casings

1. Grind the pork through the coarse disk.
2. Grind the fat through the fine disk.
3. Mix the meat and fat together and add the remaining ingredients.
4. Prepare the casings. (See Chapter 4.)
5. Stuff, tie off into eight-inch links and hang to dry for eight weeks.

---

*Prepare pork according to the instructions in Chapter 6 to assure that it is trichinosis free.

# Other Dried Sausages

## Italian-Style Dry Sausage

*This sausage is sometimes referred to as* salamette *because the links resemble a small salami. It is simple to make and can be enjoyed about six weeks after it has been hung up to dry. For ten pounds of sausage you will need:*

8 pounds lean, cubed, certified or pre-frozen pork*

2 pounds cubed pork fat*

5 tablespoons salt

1 tablespoon sugar

5 teaspoons fennel seed

2 teaspoons anise seed

1 tablespoon garlic, finely minced

2 tablespoons coarse, freshly ground black pepper

1 cup dry red wine

½ teaspoon ascorbic acid

1 teaspoon saltpeter

6 feet medium (2-inch diameter) hog casings

1. Grind meat and fat separately through the coarse disk.

2. Mix meat and fat together with the remaining ingredients.

3. Spread the mixture in a large baking pan, cover it loosely with waxed paper and cure it in the refrigerator for twenty-four hours.

4. Prepare the casings. (See Chapter 4.)

5. Stuff the meat into the casings and twist off into four-inch links. Tie off each link with cotton twine.

6. Hang the links in the prepared drying area for six to eight weeks. Test the sausage after six weeks by cutting off one link and slicing through it. If the texture is firm enough to suit your taste, the remaining sausage may be cut down and wrapped tightly for storage in the refrigerator. Prolonged drying will result in a sausage that has a texture of something like beef jerky, at which time you can either gnaw on it like a dog with a bone or use it to club intruders.

---

*Prepare pork according to the instructions in Chapter 6 to assure that it is trichinosis free.

# Pepperoni

*Pepperoni sausage is sometimes referred to as a "stick" of pepperoni because that's just about what it resembles. Most of the red color in commercial pepperoni is from paprika. Indeed, if it were from cayenne pepper you would need a fire extinguisher nearby when eating it.*

*There are many different varieties of pepperoni, some decidedly hotter than others, but most if not all rely on a beef and pork combination. All are quite pungent. Pepperoni come in different sizes, the most common being about an inch in diameter. Some commercial packers put up what they call "pizza pepperoni" which is about twice the diameter of regular pepperoni and is not as dry. This type is better able to withstand the high temperature of a baking pizza without becoming a crispy critter. If you intend to use your pepperoni primarily as a topping for pizza you might want to experiment with the drying time for best results.*

*Here are the ingredients you will need to make a ten-pound batch of pepperoni:*

**7 pounds pre-frozen or certi-fied pork butt, cubed, fat included***

**3 pounds lean beef chuck, round or shank, cubed**

**5 tablespoons salt**

**1 tablespoon sugar**

**2 tablespoons cayenne pepper**

**3 tablespoons sweet paprika**

**1 tablespoon crushed anise seed**

**1 teaspoon garlic, very finely minced**

**1 cup dry red wine**

**½ teaspoon ascorbic acid**

**1 teaspoon saltpeter**

**6 feet small (½-inch diameter) hog casings**

1. Grind the pork and beef through the coarse disk separately.

2. Mix the meats together with the remaining ingredients.

3. Spread the mixture out in a large pan, cover loosely with waxed paper, and cure in the refrigerator for twenty-four hours.

4. Prepare the casings. (See Chapter 4.)

5. Stuff the sausage into the casings and twist off into ten-inch links.

6. Using cotton twine, tie two separate knots between *every other* link, and one knot at the beginning and another at the end of the stuffed casing.

7. Cut between the double knots. This results in pairs of ten-inch links. The pepperoni are hung by a string tied to the center of each pair.

8. Hang the pepperoni to dry for six to eight weeks. Once dried, the pepperoni will keep, wrapped, in the refrigerator for several months.

*Prepare pork according to the instructions in Chapter 6 to assure that it is trichinosis free.

# Garlic Sausage

Garlic sausage is a Frenchman's steadfast friend. It is delightfully and unabashedly bourgeois, redolent with garlic and brandy. The French have a cure for the problem of garlic breath: everyone eats garlic sausage and then no one can smell the garlic on anyone else.

Garlic has been shown to have some antibiotic properties (an antibiotic is synthesized from it) and it is also a traditional remedy for high blood pressure. Shakespeare, for practical reasons no doubt, cautioned his actors from eating too much of it "to keep the breath sweet . . .", and Horace claimed it more poisonous than hemlock. But on the plus side, the Egyptian slaves wouldn't work without it, and Aristophanes claimed that it is an aphrodisiac. The ancient blind poet, Homer, credited garlic with saving Ulysses from Circe's pork barrel.

You don't have to be a scholar or historian to enjoy garlic, but I thought it might make you feel better knowing that you are in some famous company the next time you open your mouth after having eaten some garlic sausage. To make ten pounds of this potent delicacy, you will need the following:

7 pounds pre-frozen or certified pork (preferably fresh, not cured, ham), cubed*
3 pounds cubed pork fat*
5 tablespoons salt
3 tablespoons garlic, finely minced
1 cup brandy
1 tablespoon finely ground white pepper
1 teaspoon crushed bay leaf
½ teaspoon ground cloves
½ teaspoon mace
½ teaspoon dried basil leaf
½ teaspoon cinnamon
½ teaspoon dried oregano
½ teaspoon sage
½ teaspoon thyme
¼ teaspoon summer savory
¼ teaspoon cayenne pepper
1 tablespoon sweet paprika
2 tablespoons sugar
½ teaspoon ascorbic acid
1 teaspoon saltpeter
4 feet large (3½—4-inch diameter) beef casings

1. Grind the meat and fat separately through the coarse disk, mix together, and regrind through the fine disk. It will help to chill the mixture in the freezer for about thirty minutes between grindings.

2. Mix in the salt, garlic, and brandy.

3. Put the remaining dry ingredients in a blender and process until you have a fine powder.

4. Mix the powdered herb mixture into the meat.

5. Cure the meat in the refrigerator for twenty-four hours.

6. Prepare the casings. (See Chapter 4.)

7. Stuff the casings and tie off into six- or seven-inch links.

8. Hang the sausage to dry for eight to twelve weeks, or until it is sufficiently firm.

---

*Prepare pork according to the instructions in Chapter 6 to assure that it is trichinosis free.

## Summer Sausage

*You don't have to wait until summer to enjoy summer sausage. Sometimes referred to as "beef stick," this sausage is sometimes made with only beef, but a beef/pork combination packs more flavor. Traditionally, the sausage came by its name because it was prepared in the winter to last through the summer months. This recipe requires smoking, also. It tastes great with a hunk of mozzarella or Muenster cheese on a slab of French bread, washed down with a young and tender Beaujolais. Here is what you will need for ten pounds:*

**6 pounds beef chuck, including about 1 pound fat, cubed**

**4 pounds pre-frozen or certified pork, including about ½ pound fat, cubed\***

**5 tablespoons salt**

**2 tablespoons sugar**

**1 tablespoon finely ground white pepper**

**2 teaspoons crushed coriander seed**

**1 tablespoon whole black peppercorns**

**¼ teaspoon nutmeg**

**1 cup dry red wine**

**¼ teaspoon ascorbic acid**

**1 teaspoon saltpeter**

**4 feet large (3½—4-inch diameter) beef casings**

**Flavoring solution (see below)**

**¼ cup water**

**½ cup sugar**

**2 tablespoons white wine vinegar**

**1 tablespoon pure maple flavoring**

**½ teaspoon ground cloves**

**1 teaspoon pure lemon extract**

1. Grind the beef through the fine disk twice, chilling it between grindings.

2. Grind the pork through the fine blade once and mix it with the beef.

3. Make a flavoring solution with the following ingredients:

Bring the water to a boil and stir in the sugar until it is dissolved. Reduce the heat so that the liquid is barely simmering and add the remaining ingredients. Turn off the heat and allow the mixture to cool.

4. Mix the flavoring solution and all the remaining ingredients into the meat.

5. Cure the sausage in the refrigerator for twenty-four hours.

6. Prepare the casings. (See Chapter 4.)

7. Stuff the meat into the casings and tie off into six- or eight-inch links.

8. Smoke the sausage with a cool (80–90° F) smoke for about twelve hours.

9. Increase the smoke temperature to about 120° F and continue to smoke for about four or five more hours, or until the sausage is firm.

10. Let the sausage hang in a cool place at least two weeks before eating.

---

\*Prepare pork according to the instructions in Chapter 6 to assure that it is trichinosis free.

## Spanish-Style Chorizo

*You're saying we made chorizo back in the chapter on fresh sausages, and you are right. Most chorizos are sold as dry sausages, however, and that's what this recipe produces. For ten pounds you will need:*

8 pounds lean, pre-frozen or certified pork, cubed*
2 pounds pork fat, cubed*
5 tablespoons salt
2 tablespoons finely ground black pepper
3 tablespoons cayenne pepper
1 tablespoon coarsely crushed red pepper
2 tablespoons garlic, finely minced
1 teaspoon cumin seed
1 teaspoon crushed oregano
2 tablespoons sugar
1 teaspoon fennel seed
¼ cup red wine vinegar
¾ cup brandy
½ teaspoon ascorbic acid
1 teaspoon saltpeter
6 feet medium (2-inch diameter) hog casings

1. Grind the meat and fat separately through the coarse disk and mix together.
2. Sprinkle the remaining ingredients on the meat and mix thoroughly.
3. Cure the sausage in the refrigerator for twenty-four hours.
4. Prepare the casings. (See Chapter 4.)
5. Stuff the casings and tie off into four-inch links.
6. Hang the sausage to dry for about eight weeks.

## Thuringer Sausage

*This wurst is a German invention which is more often than not marketed as a fresh sausage. It is smoked slightly, and therefore will keep longer than fresh sausage, but since it is not completely dried, it should be consumed within a couple of weeks. This recipe is for five pounds.*

4 pounds lean beef, cubed
1 pound cubed pork fat*
2 tablespoons plus 1½ teaspoons salt
¼ teaspoon finely ground nutmeg
1 tablespoon finely ground white pepper

1. Grind the beef and pork fat separately through the fine disk and then mix them together.
2. Mix in the remaining ingredients.
3. Cure the mixture in the refrigerator for twenty-four hours.
4. Prepare the casings. (See Chapter 4.)
5. Stuff the meat into the casings and twist off into four- to six-inch links. Tie off the links into pairs, using two

---

*Prepare pork according to the instructions in Chapter 6 to assure that it is trichinosis free.

½ teaspoon pulverized caraway
   seed
1 tablespoon sugar
½ teaspoon crushed mustard
   seed
½ teaspoon coriander
½ teaspoon crushed coriander
½ teaspoon ground celery seed
½ teaspoon mace
2 teaspoons paprika
¼ teaspoon ascorbic acid
½ teaspoon saltpeter
4 feet medium (2-inch diameter) hog casings

separate knots between every other link, just as we did for pepperoni. Cut the pairs apart from each other.

6. Hang up the sausage to dry in a cool place, or store, uncovered, in the refrigerator for two days.

7. Bring the sausage to room temperature, and cold smoke (about 90° F) for about twelve hours.

8. Hang to dry for another day or two before eating. Make sure the sausage is kept cool.

## Garlic Ring Bologna

*Garlic ring bologna is not a fully cured sausage. It is smoked and must be kept under refrigeration until it is eaten but it will keep for a couple of weeks. To make five pounds of this sausage you will need:*

2 pounds cubed pre-frozen or
   certified pork*
1 or 2 veal hearts (about 1
   pound total)
2 pounds pork fat, cubed*
5 teaspoons salt
2 teaspoons finely ground
   white pepper
2 teaspoons crushed mustard
   seed
1 teaspoon marjoram
1 teaspoon ground allspice
4 cloves garlic, very finely
   minced
¼ teaspoon ascorbic acid
½ teaspoon saltpeter
4 feet medium (2-inch diameter) hog casings

1. Grind the pork, veal heart, and fat separately through the fine disk.

2. Mix the meats and fat together with the remaining ingredients.

3. Chill the mixture, and then regrind through the fine disk.

4. Prepare the casings. (See Chapter 4.)

5. Stuff the casings and twist off into eighteen-inch links. Be careful not to overstuff, or when you form the rings, the casings may burst. Tie double knots between the links and separate them. Bring the tied ends of each link together and tie securely, forming a ring.

6. Hang the sausage in a cool drying area, or place in the refrigerator for eight to ten hours, uncovered.

7. Smoke at 110-120° F for about two hours.

8. Bring a large pot of water to a bare simmer, about 180-190° F.

9. Simmer the rings for twenty to thirty minutes. When done, they should float to the surface.

10. Cool and store refrigerated for up to two weeks.

---

*Prepare pork according to the instructions in Chapter 6 to assure that it is trichinosis free.

## Mettwurst

*This delicious German sausage is smoked and precooked but, like ring bologna, it must be kept refrigerated, and can be stored for up to two weeks. To make five pounds of mettwurst you will need:*

3 pounds lean beef chuck, cubed

2 pounds pre-frozen or certified pork butt with fat, cubed*

5 teaspoons salt

1 teaspoon finely ground white pepper

½ teaspoon ground nutmeg

½ teaspoon ground celery seed

½ teaspoon ground allspice

¼ teaspoon freshly ground ginger root

¼ teaspoon ground marjoram

¼ teaspoon ascorbic acid

½ teaspoon saltpeter

4 feet medium (2-inch diameter) hog casings

1. Grind both meats through the fine disk separately and then mix them together.
2. Mix the remaining ingredients with the meat.
3. Prepare the casings. (See Chapter 4.)
4. Stuff the mixture into the casings and tie off into six-inch links.
5. Cure in the refrigerator for twenty-four hours.
6. Smoke at about 110-120° F for two hours, and then raise the temperature to 150° F and smoke for two more hours.
7. Simmer in a kettle of 180-190° F water for thirty minutes. The sausages should rise to the top when they are done.
8. Place the mettwurst in a kettle of cool water for thirty minutes, remove, dry thoroughly, and refrigerate for up to two weeks.

## Braunschweiger

*This German sausage is made from pure pork, is mildly spiced, and has a distinctive smoky flavor. The pork liver in the recipe lends its own special taste to the sausage. For five pounds:*

2½ pounds pre-frozen or certified pork liver, trimmed and cubed*

2½ pounds pre-frozen or certified pork butt with fat, cubed*

½ cup ice water

¼ cup nonfat dry milk

5 teaspoons salt

1 tablespoon sugar

2 tablespoons finely minced onion

1. Grind the liver and the pork butt separately through the fine disk and then mix them together.
2. Add the remaining ingredients, mix well, and chill in the freezer for thirty minutes. Regrind through the fine disk.
3. Prepare the casings. (See Chapter 4.)
4. Stuff into casings and tie off into six- or eight-inch links.
5. Simmer in a large kettle of 180-190° F water for an hour.
6. Remove the sausage from the water, dry thoroughly, and smoke at 150° F for two hours.

*Prepare pork according to the instructions in Chapter 6 to assure that it is trichinosis free.

2 teaspoons finely ground
     white pepper
1 teaspoon crushed mustard
     seed
½ teaspoon ground marjoram
¼ teaspoon ground allspice
¼ teaspoon ascorbic acid
½ teaspoon saltpeter
4 feet medium (2-inch diam-
     eter) hog casings

7. Place the braunschweiger in a large pot of cool water for thirty minutes, remove, dry, and store in the refrigerator for up to two weeks.

## Smoked Kielbasa

*In Chapter 5, we made fresh Polish sausage. This smoked version is closer to what you find in the grocer's meatcase. In the spring, this sausage is sometimes referred to as "Easter sausage." When you see it labeled as such, saunter over to the cooler because you are also apt to find another springtime treat—bock beer. Bock beer is a traditional spring beer because in the old days brewers would clean out their vats and use the sludge at the bottom to make a dark, heavy, sweetish brew. Bock beer, rye bread, and smoked kielbasa are perfect partners. To make five pounds of this sausage, you will need the following:*

3 pounds pre-frozen or certi-
     fied pork butt, with fat,
     cubed*
2 pounds beef chuck, trimmed
     and cubed
½ cup ice water
¼ cup nonfat dry milk
5 teaspoons salt
1 tablespoon sugar
1 tablespoon paprika
2 teaspoons finely ground
     white pepper
1 tablespoon garlic, finely
     minced
½ teaspoon ground marjoram
½ teaspoon ground thyme
½ teaspoon ground celery seed
½ teaspoon finely ground cor-
     iander
½ teaspoon freshly ground nut-
     meg
¼ teaspoon ascorbic acid
½ teaspoon saltpeter
4 feet medium (2-inch diam-
     eter) hog casings

1. Grind the pork through the coarse disk.
2. Grind the beef through the fine disk.
3. Mix the meats together and mix with the remaining ingredients.
4. Prepare the casings. (See Chapter 4.)
5. Stuff the mixture into the casings and tie off into eight- to ten-inch links.
6. Cure in the refrigerator for twenty-four hours.
7. Smoke at 180–190° F for two hours.
8. Bring a large kettle of water to a temperature of 170–180° F and simmer the sausage for half an hour.
9. Place the links in a kettle of cool water for half an hour, dry, and store in the refrigerator for up to two weeks.

---

*Prepare pork according to the instructions in Chapter 6 to assure that it is trichinosis free.

## Smoked Country-Style Sausage

*Sometimes you will see something similar to this sausage in the fresh meat case at the grocery, labeled "smoked country links." It is delicious both as a breakfast sausage or as part of an hors d'oeuvres selection. This recipe makes five pounds.*

**3 pounds pre-frozen or certified pork butt, cubed***
**2 pounds beef chuck, about ¼ fat, cubed**
**½ cup ice water**
**¼ cup nonfat dry milk**
**5 teaspoons salt**
**1 tablespoon sugar**
**1 tablespoon paprika**
**2 teaspoons finely ground white pepper**
**2 teaspoons mustard seed**
**¼ teaspoon ascorbic acid**
**½ teaspoon saltpeter**
**4 feet small (1-inch diameter) hog or sheep casings**

1. Grind the pork through the fine disk.
2. Grind the beef through the coarse disk.
3. Mix the meats together, add the remaining ingredients and mix through well.
4. Prepare the casings. (See Chapter 4.)
5. Stuff the meat mixture into the casings and tie off into two- to three-inch links.
6. Smoke for two hours at 180–190° F.
7. Simmer in 190° F water for thirty minutes.
8. Remove to a kettle of cool water for half an hour, dry, and store in the refrigerator for up to two weeks.

## Bavarian Summer Sausage

*In one sense, this isn't a true summer sausage because it has to be refrigerated for longer storage since it isn't as dry as most sausages that claim the name "summer sausage." In another sense, though, it is as summery a sausage as you can find because it goes beautifully with a stein of ice-cold German lager, rye bread, and a shady tree on a sultry summer afternoon. For five pounds:*

**4 pounds beef chuck, with fat cubed**
**1 pound pre-frozen or certified pork butt, with fat, cubed***
**5 teaspoons salt**
**2 tablespoons sugar**
**1 tablespoon whole mustard seed**
**2 teaspoons finely ground white pepper**
**¼ teaspoon ascorbic acid**
**½ teaspoon saltpeter**
**4 feet medium (2-inch diameter) hog casings**

1. Grind the beef and pork separately through the fine disk.
2. Mix the meats together with the remaining ingredients.
3. Prepare the casings. (See Chapter 4.)
4. Stuff the mixture into the casings and tie off into four-inch links.
5. Smoke at 140° F for four hours or until the sausage is firm to the touch; increase the temperature to 180–190° F, and continue smoking for two hours.
6. Cool and refrigerate.

---

*Prepare pork according to the instructions in Chapter 6 to assure that it is trichinosis free.

## Smoked Italian-Style Links

*These sausages have a decidedly different flavor than other Italian-style sausages. The simplicity of the recipe is seductively deceptive: the thyme and rosemary combine with the complex herbal base of the sweet vermouth and smokey flavor to produce an aromatic and sophisticated sausage which is hard to stop eating once you've started. Fresh French bread and a dry red wine are excellent foils to the sweetish pungency of the meat. For five pounds:*

**3 pounds pre-frozen or certified pork butt, with fat, cubed***

**2 pounds beef chuck, fat included, cubed**

**5 teaspoons salt**

**3 tablespoons paprika**

**2 teaspoons thyme**

**2 teaspoons rosemary**

**1 teaspoon nutmeg**

**½ cup sweet vermouth**

**¼ teaspoon ascorbic acid**

**½ teaspoon saltpeter**

**4 feet medium (2-inch diameter) hog casings**

1. Grind the pork through the coarse disk.
2. Grind the beef through the fine disk.
3. Mix the meats together with the remaining ingredients.
4. Prepare the casings. (See Chapter 4.)
5. Stuff the casings and tie off into four- or five-inch links.
6. Smoke for about two hours at 180–190° F.
7. Bring a large kettle of water to a boil, reduce heat to maintain a water temperature of 170–180° F, and simmer the sausage for thirty minutes.
8. Cool and store under refrigeration.

*Prepare pork according to the instructions in Chapter 6 to assure that it is trichinosis free.

## Czech Yirtrnička

*Italy, France, and Germany are divided into many regions within their national boundaries, and each region has contributed many unique and exciting dishes to the ethnic cuisine of its country. Many people don't know that Czechoslovakia is also divided into three distinct regions: Moravia, Bohemia, and Slovakia. Each region has its own distinctive cuisine.*

*Once a part of the Austro–Hungarian Empire, the area which we call Czechoslovakia is really an infant country in terms of European history. Czechoslavakia's political birthdate goes back only as far as 1918 when, as a result of the postwar turmoil, the Slovaks voted to join in union with the Czechs of Bohemia and Moravia. The union has traditionally been a very uneasy one, troubled by racial problems and the proliferation of political parties to which these problems give rise. Czech national heritage is more a part of political compromise than national unity. Culturally, Bohemia and Moravia have no more in common with Slovakia than Sicily has with Naples.*

It is not necessary to understand Czech history to appreciate the country's culinary traditions any more than it is necessary to appreciate the sterling beauty of fine Bohemian crystal and lace. An appreciation of Czechoslovakia's cultural history, however, does help one understand why Czech blood sausage, liver sausage, and wine sausage (klobasy as opposed to kielbasa) are different from their German, Austrian, and Polish counterparts.

This recipe for yirtrničky is Moravian, owing to my grandparents' cultural heritage. There are no doubt many other delicious versions of this sausage since many villages within the separate regions of Czechoslovakia have their own versions based upon family recipes handed down from one generation to the next. Regardless of the peculiarities of a given recipe, they all rely on one basic premise: to make absolutely authentic yirtrničky, you need access to a freshly butchered pig. If you raise your own hogs, then you are ready to roll (or stuff, as the case may be), but if you are like most people today, you are going to have to get real friendly with your butcher so that you can impose upon him for some rather exotic cuts of pork. Many meat shops today get their meat shipped to them in primal cuts (loin, shoulder, etc.), neatly packaged in vacuum-packed plastic bags. It is likely that some modern meat cutters have never seen an entire freshly butchered animal carcass. Find one who still does things the old-fashioned way.

Once you've become friendly with an old-fashioned butcher, screw up your courage and with the biggest smile you can muster, ask him for a pig's head and the lungs, heart, and kidneys from a single carcass. While you're at it, also ask for half of a freshly sliced pork liver. Contrary to what you might think, he probably won't laugh at you. Instead he will probably admire your initiative. With your shopping cart loaded with these exotic cuts, you are ready to make a most delectable sausage. Because this recipe does not use standard, easily measurable cuts of meat, you are going to have to improvise somewhat. But bear with me—the results are worth the effort.*

For one batch of yirtrničky, here is what you will need:

**1 pig head**
**1 pair of lungs**
**1 pork heart**
**2 pork kidneys**
**½ pork liver, freshly sliced**

So far this recipe looks like something you might expect to find in a medieval manual for prospective homemakers, but it gets easier.

1. In a very large kettle, boil the pig's head for four or five hours or until the meat begins to fall from the bone.

---

*No two pig's heads are exactly the same and neither are the internal organs, so you will have to juggle the other ingredients somewhat according to these directions.

Stale bread
Salt
Fine ground black pepper
Ground allspice
Ground cloves
Grated lemon rind
Marjoram
Several cloves of garlic, finely
  minced
Ascorbic acid
Saltpeter
Hog casings, medium size
  (2-inch diameter)

2. While the head is merrily (but gently) bubbling away, in a separate kettle boil the lungs, heart, and kidneys for about two hours or until the meat is tender.

3. Chill the liver slices in the freezer for half an hour and, after cutting them into cubes, put them through the coarse disk of the meat grinder.

4. When the head and organs are cooked and cool enough to handle, scrape all the meat from the head, cube the organs, mix all with the raw liver, and put this through the fine disk.

5. Determine how much meat you have (use a measuring cup) and for each part meat, combine with two parts of stale white bread that has been soaked in water and then squeezed dry.

6. Here comes the tricky part: weigh the entire mixture on a kitchen scale to determine the amount of seasonings you are going to need. If you don't have a kitchen scale, weigh yourself on the bathroom scale, weigh yourself again while you are holding the meat mixture, and subtract the first figure from the second one. Don't forget to figure in the weight of the container. (This method has the obvious disadvantage of reminding you of the fact that you should probably be out jogging instead of making more goodies to eat.)

7. Having determined the weight of the sausage mixture, add the following ingredients in the proportions listed: 1 teaspoon salt per pound, one-half teaspoon black pepper per pound, one-quarter teaspoon each of allspice and cloves per pound, and one-half teaspoon marjoram, grated lemon rind and minced garlic per pound. Add ascorbic acid at the rate of one-quarter teaspoon per five pounds and saltpeter at the rate of one teaspoon per ten pounds.

8. Prepare the casings. (See Chapter 4.)

9. Stuff the casings and tie off into six-inch links.

10. Bring a large kettle of water to a boil, reduce to a simmer, and cook the links until they rise to the top. Don't let the water boil once the links have been added, or they may burst.

11. Cool the sausage in a pot of cool water, remove it, and pat it dry.

12. You can refrigerate the sausage and eat it cold, or warm it up at a later date. Or, you can smoke it at about 120° F for about four hours, or until it is very firm.

Congratulations! Once you have mastered the recipes in this chapter, you qualify for the title *wurstmacher*!

# Chapter 8

# Poultry Sausages

**W**hen one thinks of sausage, the meat that ordinarily comes to mind is pork, sometimes beef, but usually never meat that comes from anything that has wings and feathers. There are probably more recipes dealing with what you can do with whole poultry or poultry pieces, especially chicken, than with any other kind of meat. But sausage?

Why not?

Poultry is one of the most healthful foods around. Ounce for ounce, it is a treasure house of protein and minerals and an absolute bargain when one compares the proportion of lean to fat meat. Chicken and turkey especially are recommended for people on low fat and/or low calorie diets.

All poultry has the added advantage of being a rather bland meat. This means that we can do just about anything to it to make it taste as we please.

One person who has studied the possiblities of what can be done with poultry is Dr. Robert C. Baker of the New York State College of Agriculture and Life Sciences at Cornell University. Dr. Baker is the inventor of the so-called "chicken dog."

In an attempt to find new uses for poultry, especially laying hens past their prime, Dr. Baker and his colleagues found that one can do just about anything with chicken and turkey that one can do with red meat. And poultry has the advantage of being cheaper and lower in fat than red meat.

Lest anyone doubt that a chicken dog can taste like a "real" hot dog, sensory analysis of products developed by Dr. Baker and his colleagues has proven that people are just as apt to like a product made from chicken or turkey meat, even though it may be a traditionally red meat product. The proliferation at the corner deli of things like "turkey salami," "turkey pastrami," or "chicken bologna," are proof that the public is readily willing to accept these products made from poultry. Large companies would not invest the capital necessary to produce these products if the public did not accept them.

Although Dr. Baker's work extends beyond what the home sausage maker might find valuable, it does open up possibilities that anyone with a food grinder and a source of poultry will find exciting.

# Sausage Recipes

Because everyone's tastes are different, these recipes are meant to be guides or starting points for the home sausage maker. Generally speaking, a larger proportion of dark meat (or even all dark meat) produces a somewhat more pleasing sausage than one from predominantly white or all white meat. Dark meat has a slightly higher fat content which a successful sausage needs. Remember, we're talking chicken and turkey here, so the fat content is already at bargain basement levels.

As we noted earlier, poultry tends to be a bland meat. Generally speaking, a sausage made from chicken or turkey will need a little more spice than would a similar sausage made from red meat. When making poultry sausages for the first time, use these recipes as a guideline, but don't be afraid to be creative. Like more fennel in your Italian sausage? More garlic in your kielbasa? Try it. You'll probably like it!

One final word: what about skin and added fat? Commercial sausages made from chicken and turkey meat do contain the skin and fat normally found on a whole bird. The inclusion of these two ingredients improve both taste and texture. Generally, I have found that the addition of some skin greatly improves the sausage. Since we are talking about an essentially lean meat to begin with, when compared with red meat, the addition of a small amount of fat seems an acceptable price to pay for a more palatable sausage. But the decision is yours. If you are willing to sacrifice something in taste and texture for an even leaner product, go right ahead. In the following recipes, when a recipe specifies, for example, 4 pounds of chicken, it presumes that about fifteen percent of that is skin and fat. Experiment with the proportions to suit your and your family's individual tastes and needs. After all, isn't that one of the reasons you are making your own sausage to begin with?

## Chicken Bratwurst

*This is a mildly flavored sausage, perfect as an anchor for a "lite" meal.*

3 feet small (1½-inch diameter) hog or sheep casings
3 pounds chicken meat
½ teaspoon allspice
¾ teaspoon caraway seeds, crushed
¾ teaspoon dried marjoram
1 teaspoon finely ground white pepper
1 teaspoon salt, or to taste

1. Prepare the casings. (See Chapter 4.)
2. Grind the meat through the small disk.
3. Mix the remaining ingredients with the meat. Chill the mixture for thirty minutes in the refrigerator.
4. Grind through the small disk and stuff into casings. Refrigerate for up to two days or freeze.

## Chicken Dog #1

*This is a recipe for a "fresh" (uncured) chicken frankfurter like the one found in Chapter 5.*

3 feet small hog (1½-inch diameter) or sheep casings
3 pounds chicken meat
1 tablespoon onion powder
1 teaspoon garlic powder
1 teaspoon finely ground coriander
½ teaspoon dried marjoram
½ teaspoon ground mace
½ teaspoon finely ground mustard seed
1 teaspoon paprika
1 teaspoon finely ground white pepper
1 teaspoon sugar
1½ teaspoons salt

1. Prepare the casings. (See Chapter 4.)
2. Mix the remaining ingredients together with the meat.
3. If you desire a more sausage like texture to your hot dog, grind the mixture through the fine disk twice and stuff into casings.
4. If you desire a more emulsified texture like that found in commercially manufactured hot dogs, put the meat and seasonings mixture, about a third at a time, in the bowl of a food processor. Process until the mixture is a thick puree-like consistency. The result is somewhat harder to stuff into casings but, when cooked, it closely resembles that of a "real" hot dog.
5. Twist off the sausage into five-inch links.
6. Bring a large pot of water to a boil. Add the links (without separating them), immediately reduce the heat and simmer *very* gently for thirty minutes.
7. Remove the franks and place them in ice water. Chill thoroughly.
8. Remove, pat dry, and refrigerate. Chicken dogs can be stored up to a week under refrigeration.

# Chicken Dog #2

*This recipe makes what most people would call a "hot dog" because the meat is cured.*

5 feet small hog (1½-inch diameter) or sheep casings
5 pounds chicken meat
1 cup nonfat dry milk
1 tablespoon onion powder
1 teaspoon garlic powder
2 teaspoons finely ground coriander
1 teaspoon dried majoram
1 teaspoon ground mace
1 teaspoon finely ground mustard seed
1 tablespoon paprika
1 tablespoon sugar
¼ teaspoon ascorbic acid
Either 3 teaspoons salt and ½ teaspoon saltpeter
Or 5 teaspoons of commercial meat cure, such as Morton's Tender Quick (containing 0.5% sodium nitrite and 0.5% sodium nitrate)

1. Prepare the casings. (See Chapter 4.)
2. Mix the chicken with all remaining ingredients.
3. Grind the mixture through the coarse disk. Chill for thirty minutes in the refrigerator.
4. Grind the mixture through the fine disk. Chill for thirty minutes.
5. Grind the mixture a second time through the fine disk and stuff into casings. Twist off into five-inch links.
6. Smoke the links in a cool smoke for two hours.
7. Steam or simmer the links for thirty minutes or until they are cooked through.
8. Cook, pat dry, and refrigerate. Allow to cure for three days before heating and eating.

# Country Chicken Sausage

*This sausage relies on the traditional "country sausage" combination of herbs and spices, sage, thyme, ginger, and savory.*

2 feet small (1½-inch diameter) hog or sheep casings
2 pounds chicken meat
1 teaspoon salt, or to taste
1 teaspoon freshly ground black pepper
½ teaspoon ground sage
½ teaspoon ground thyme
½ teaspoon ground ginger
½ teaspoon summer savory
½ teaspoon cayenne pepper (optional)

1. Prepare the casings. (See Chapter 4.)
2. Grind the chicken through the fine disk.
3. Mix the chicken with the remaining ingredients.
4. Grind the mixture through the fine disk and stuff into the casings. Twist off into two- to three-inch links.
5. To cook, sauté in vegetable oil until evenly browned and cooked through.

## Roman-Style Chicken Sausage

*This sausage comes by its name from that classic trio of Roman flavorings: onions, sweet peppers, and freshly grated Romano cheese.*

4 feet small (1½-inch diameter) hog or sheep casings
4 pounds chicken meat
2 teaspoons salt, or to taste
2 teaspoons coarsely ground black pepper
1 cup onion, finely chopped
½ cup sweet green pepper, finely chopped
½ cup freshly grated Romano cheese

1. Prepare the casings. (See Chapter 4.)
2. Grind the chicken through the coarse disk.
3. Mix the chicken with the remaining ingredients.
4. Grind the mixture through the coarse disk and stuff into the casings. Twist off into four-inch links.
5. To cook, sauté in vegetable oil until evenly browned and cooked through.

## Sicilian-Style Turkey Sausage

*Sicilian sausages rely principally upon fennel seed for their distinctive flavor and this variation is no exception.*

5 feet small hog (1½-inch diameter) or sheep casings
5 pounds turkey meat
2 teaspoons whole fennel seed
2 teaspoons crushed fennel seed
2 teaspoons crushed red pepper (optional)
2 teaspoons salt, or to taste
2 teaspoons freshly ground black pepper
1 teaspoon garlic powder *or* 2 cloves garlic, very finely minced

1. Prepare the casings. (See Chapter 4.)
2. Grind the turkey through the fine disk.
3. Mix the turkey with the remaining ingredients.
4. Grind the mixture through the fine disk and stuff into casings. Twist off into three-inch links.
5. To cook, sauté the links in vegetable oil until they are evenly browned.

# Turkey Chorizo

*Turkey may be a rather bland meat but this sausage is no shrinking violet. As in all chorizo-style sausages, hot red pepper carries the day here.*

5 feet small hog (1½-inch diameter) or sheep casings
5 pounds turkey meat
2 teaspoons oregano
2 teaspoons cumin
1 teaspoon freshly ground cinnamon
1 teaspoon ground coriander
1 teaspoon ground ginger
2 tablespoons sweet paprika
2 teaspoons cayenne pepper
½ teaspoon celery seed
¼ cup dry red wine
2 teaspoons freshly ground black pepper
2 teaspoons salt, or to taste

1. Prepare the casings. (See Chapter 4.)
2. Grind the turkey through the fine disk.
3. Mix the turkey with the remaining ingredients.
4. Grind the turkey through the fine disk and stuff into the casings. Twist off into three-inch links.
5. Sauté in vegetable oil until evenly browned and cooked through.

# Garlic Turkey Sausage

*For a more pungent garlic flavor in this sausage, you can increase the amount of fresh garlic, or simply use the amount of garlic powder the recipe specifies. Garlic powder, because it is dehydrated, lacks the fresh taste of garlic cloves but it packs more of a garlic punch.*

5 feet small hog (1½-inch diameter) or sheep casings
5 pounds turkey
1 tablespoon ground coriander seed
2 teaspoons salt, or to taste
2 teaspoons freshly ground black pepper
1 teaspoon garlic powder *or* 2 cloves garlic, finely minced

1. Prepare the casings. (See Chapter 4.)
2. Grind the turkey through the fine disk.
3. Mix the turkey with the remaining ingredients.
4. Grind the mixture through the fine disk and stuff into the casings. Twist off into three-inch links.
5. To cook, sauté in vegetable oil until evenly browned and cooked through.

## Duck Kielbasa

*Ducks and geese differ from chickens and turkeys in that their fat is incorporated in their skin, whereas the fat in chicken and turkey is more or less a separate entity between the skin and the meat. Except for a few small fat deposits near the thighs and breasts, most of the fat in a chicken or turkey is in a large cluster around the vent of the bird, thus making it easy to remove should one desire.*

*Because of the nature of the fat deposits in ducks and geese, depending upon how they are prepared, dishes made from them can be quite high in fat. In making sausage from ducks and geese, however, we can control the amount in the final product to a great extent by controlling how much of the skin and its attendant fat finds its way into the sausage. Remember, some fat is necessary for taste and texture.*

4 feet small hog (1½-inch diameter)

4 pounds domestic duck

2 teaspoons salt, or to taste

2 teaspoons freshly ground black pepper

2 teaspoons garlic powder, *or* 4 cloves garlic, very finely minced

1 teaspoon marjoram

1 teaspoon summer savory

½ teaspoon allspice

1 tablespoon sweet paprika

1. Prepare the casings. (See Chapter 4.)
2. Grind the duck through the fine disk.
3. Mix the duck with the remaining ingredients.
4. Grind the mixture through the fine disk and stuff into the casings. Twist off into three- or four-inch links.
5. To cook, sauté in a small amount of vegetable oil until evenly browned and cooked through.

## Bohemian Duck Sausage

*Although it is somewhat more assertive than chicken, domestic duck meat really has a mild flavor which is high-lighted by the combination of herbs in this recipe.*

4 feet small hog (1½-inch diameter) or sheep casings

4 pounds domestic duck meat

2 teaspoons salt, or to taste

2 teaspoons white pepper

1 teaspoon celery seed

1 teaspoon mustard seed

1 teaspoon chervil

1 teaspoon tarragon

1. Prepare the casings. (See Chapter 4.)
2. Grind the duck through the coarse disk.
3. Mix the duck with the remaining ingredients.
4. Grind the mixture through the fine disk and stuff into the casings. Twist off into three- or four-inch links.
5. To cook, sauté in vegetable oil until evenly browned and cooked through.

# Goosewurst

*Whether you use fresh or frozen goose meat, this may be one of the best* wursts *you've ever tasted.*

5 feet medium (2-inch diameter) hog casings
5 pounds goose meat
½ cup *Drambuie* (Scotch liqueur)
2 teaspoons salt, or to taste
2 teaspoons freshly ground white pepper
½ cup very finely chopped onion
¼ cup chopped fresh chives
1 teaspoon mace
1 teaspoon ground coriander
½ teaspoon cayenne pepper
1 tablespoon sweet paprika

1. Prepare the casings. (See Chapter 4.)
2. Grind the goose through the coarse disk.
3. Pour the *Drambuie* over the goose, mix well, and refrigerate for at least three hours or overnight.
4. Mix the goose with the remaining ingredients.
5. Grind the mixture through the fine disk and stuff into the casings. Twist off into three- or four-inch links.
6. To cook, sauté in vegetable oil until evenly browned and cooked through.

# Chapter 9

# Fish Sausages

**S**campi sausage?

As strange as the idea might seem, a perfectly delicious, appetizing, and appealing sausage can indeed be made from fish.

But why bother? The reasons are simple. Fish is good for you. It is low in fat (and recent studies indicate that fish that is relatively higher in fat may be even better for you). It can be very economical. Underutilized species of fish sell at reasonable prices. Just recently on a tour through my local supermarket, flounder was selling for $7.00 a pound, but pollock, a perfectly desirable fish, was on special for less than $2.00 a pound. In fact, frozen pollock was at its regular price of $1.69 a pound. And there is no waste.

And most importantly, fish is delicious. It is also amenable to just about any treatment that one might wish to give it.

When making sausages from fish there are a couple of things that we must keep in mind. First of all, it isn't necessary to spend a fortune on shrimp or lobster or other expensive species to make a shrimp or lobster sausage. The reason is that most white fish have a bonding property when minced and cooked that will serve as a vehicle for the more expensive ingredients in our sausage.

Second, there is practically no waste, especially when using fish fillets, and therefore one can make less than one would when using meat and still have plenty of finished product to serve the same number of people.

One additional note: it helps to have a food processor if you plan on making fish sausages. Fish can be ground in a food grinder, but the procedure for making fish sausage is greatly simplified by using a processor.

As with all recipes in this book, consider the ones that follow as guides or starting points. Experiment with quantities and varieties of spices to suit your individual tastes. When making a batch of sausage, cook up a spoonful of your seasoned mixture to taste for seasonings, and adjust them to suit your fancy.

Although the following recipes give instructions for stuffing the sausages into casings, perfectly acceptable sausage can be made by shaping the seasoned mixture into patties.

Cooking instructions for all the sausage are basically the same. They may be steamed, baked (covered), or microwaved. They can also be sautéed in a little vegetable oil or butter. Just remember that we're dealing with fish, and fish doesn't take a long time to cook.

One final note: recipes that specify "whitefish" mean you can use practically any white fleshed fish that is reasonably priced.

# Sausage Recipes

## Old Bay Sausage

*Because of the neutral taste of the fish in this recipe, the seasonings are essentially what you taste. You might try this one if your family isn't fond of fish because unless you tell them what they are eating, they probably won't be able to guess.*

**4 feet small (1½-inch diameter) hog casings**
**2 pounds whitefish fillet, thawed if frozen**
**1 egg, beaten**
**½ teaspoon celery salt**
**¼ teaspoon crushed mustard seed**
**¼ teaspoon finely ground black pepper**
**¼ teaspoon ground bay leaf**
**¼ teaspoon ground cloves**
**¼ teaspoon ground ginger**
**¼ teaspoon mace**
**¼ teaspoon cardamom**
**1 teaspoon sweet paprika**
**1 teaspoon lemon juice**

1. Prepare the casings. (See Chapter 4.)
2. Cut the fish into two-inch cubes and process in a food processor until the fish is just broken, about three on/off cycles.
3. Add the remaining ingredients and process just until everything is well blended.
4. Stuff the mixture into casings and twist off into three- to four-inch links.

# Fresh Herb Sausage

*The fresh chives and parsley give this sausage a distinctive flavor.*

4 feet small (1½-inch diameter) hog casings
2 pounds whitefish fillet, thawed if frozen, cubed
1 egg, beaten
2 tablespoons chopped fresh chives
1 tablespoon chopped fresh parsley
1 teaspoon lemon juice
½ teaspoon celery salt
½ teaspoon finely ground black pepper

1. Prepare the casings. (See Chapter 4.)
2. Put the fish in the bowl of a food processor and process just until the fish is broken, about three on/off cycles.
3. Add the remaining ingredients and process just until everything is well blended.
4. Stuff the mixture into casings and twist off into three- to four-inch links.

# Lobster Sausage

*There's no need to take out a second mortgage on the family homestead since lobster only accounts for a small portion of the ingredients in this recipe. The distinctive flavor of the lobster meat, however, perfumes the entire sausage.*

4 feet small (1½-inch diameter) hog casings
1½ pounds whitefish fillet, thawed if frozen, cubed
½ teaspoon ground mustard seed
½ teaspoon ground coriander
1 teaspoon paprika
1 teaspoon lemon juice
½ teaspoon freshly ground white pepper
1 egg, beaten
½ pound lobster meat, coarsely chopped

1. Prepare the casings. (See Chapter 4.)
2. Process the fish in a food processor just until it is broken, about three on/off cycles.
3. Add the mustard, coriander, paprika, lemon juice, pepper, and egg. Process until blended.
4. Put the mixture in a mixing bowl and add the lobster meat. Mix through well.
5. Stuff the mixture into casings and twist off into three- to four-inch links.

## Shrimp Sausage

*Fresh or frozen shrimp are best in this recipe, however you can use canned shrimp. Just be sure to rinse them well under cold running water to get rid of the slight "tinny" taste that canned seafood sometimes acquires.*

**4 feet small (1½-inch diameter) hog casings**
**1½ pounds white fish fillet, thawed if frozen, cubed.**
**1 egg, beaten**
**1 teaspoon onion powder**
**1 teaspoon sweet paprika**
**1 teaspoon lemon juice**
**2 tablespoons chopped parsley**
**½ pound very small shrimp, peeled and deveined**

1. Prepare the casings. (See Chapter 4.)
2. Process the fish in a food processor just until it is broken, about three on/off cycles.
3. Add the egg, onion powder, paprika, lemon juice, and parsley. Process until well blended.
4. Put the fish mixture into a mixing bowl and add the shrimp. Mix through well.
5. Stuff into casings and tie off into three- to four-inch links.

## Clam Dogs

*A "Down East" favorite is the "clamwhich,"—fried clams heaped into a New England style toasted hot dog bun and topped with tartar sauce. You might try eating your clam dogs in the same manner.*

**4 feet small (1½-inch diameter) hog casings**
**1½ pounds whitefish fillet, thawed, cubed**
**1 egg, beaten**
**2 tablespoons chopped parsley**
**1 teaspoon onion powder**
**1 teaspoon garlic powder**
**½ teaspoon coarsely ground black pepper**
**½ teaspoon basil**
**1 teaspoon lemon juice**
**2 six ounce cans chopped clams, drained**

1. Prepare the casings. (See Chapter 4.)
2. Process the fish in a food processor just until it is broken, about three on/off cycles.
3. Add the remaining ingredients except the clams. Process until blended.
4. Put the fish mixture in a mixing bowl and add the clams. Mix through well.
5. Stuff into casings and twist off into three- to four-inch links.

## Scampi Sausage

*In Italian, scampi means shrimp. In this country, however, the term usually refers to a dish made with lots of garlic and butter.*

4 feet small (1½-inch diameter) hog casings

1 pound white fish fillet, thawed if frozen, cubed

2 eggs, beaten

1 teaspoon vegetable oil

1 teaspoon butter, melted

1 teaspoon lemon juice

1 teaspoon onion powder

1 tablespoon garlic, finely minced

½ teaspoon allspice

½ pound very small shrimp, peeled and deveined

¼ pound crab meat, shredded

¼ pound bay scallops, quartered

1. Prepare the casings. (See Chapter 4.)

2. Process the fish in a food processor just until it is broken, about three on/off cycles.

3. Add the eggs, oil, butter, lemon juice, onion powder, garlic, and allspice. Process until well blended.

4. Add the shrimp, crab, and scallops. Process just until blended. Do not over process.

5. Stuff the mixture into casings and twist off into three- to four-inch links.

## Conch Sausage

*The conch is a marine mollusk probably best known for its attractive shell which people put up to their ear to hear the sound of the sea. Although you could use fresh conch in this recipe, it is more practical to use the canned variety because it is more readily available and does not need to be tenderized, as does the fresh, since the canning process handles that process eminently well.*

4 feet small (1½-inch diameter) hog casings

1½ pounds whitefish fillet, thawed if frozen, cubed

1 egg, beaten

1 teaspoon crushed red pepper flakes

½ teaspoon oregano

½ teaspoon rosemary

1 teaspoon lemon juice

2 six ounce cans conch, drained

1. Prepare the casings. (See Chapter 4.)

2. Process the fish just until it is broken, about three on/off cycles.

3. Add the egg, red pepper, oregano, rosemary, and lemon juice. Process until well blended. Remove the mixture to a mixing bowl.

4. Add the conch to the processor, and process until the conch is the texture of minced clams. Add the conch to the fish mixture and mix through well.

5. Stuff the mixture into casings and twist off into three- to four-inch links.

## Squid Sausage

*This is a very unique sausage in that the "casing" is the body of the squid. You may be familiar with the Mediterranean dish of stuffed squid, from which this recipe derives. Squid has virtually no flavor in and of itself. If you wanted to experiment, you could use the technique here for any of the other sausages in this chapter. They wouldn't look like ordinary sausages, but they would certainly taste delicious. This recipe makes enough for four people.*

8 medium squid, about 6–7 inches long
1 clove garlic, finely minced
1 cup chopped fresh parsley
½ teaspoon oregano
1 teaspoon salt, or to taste
1 teaspoon coarsely ground black pepper
1 cup fresh bread crumbs
1 tablespoon plus ¼ cup olive oil
½ cup dry vermouth
2 cups crushed tomatoes

1. To clean the squid: cut off the tentacles and reserve. Cut off and discard the mouth which is in the center of the tentacles. Under cold running water, peel off the outer skin and discard. Squeeze the body to push out the insides, pulling off the head when the insides are out. Pull out the center bone (it looks like a piece of clear plastic) and discard. Turn the body inside out and rinse well. Turn back and rinse. Dry on paper towels.

2. Chop the tentacles coarsely in a food processor. Add the garlic, parsley, oregano, salt, and pepper. Process until blended.

3. Add the bread crumbs and one tablespoon of the olive oil. Mix well.

4. Fill the bodies of the squid. Fill between half- and three-quarters full. If you over fill them, they will burst when they cook.

5. Either skewer them shut with toothpicks or roughly stitch them closed with cotton thread and a needle.

6. Heat the quarter cup of olive oil in a skillet and add the squid. Turn often to prevent them from sticking. Cook until lightly browned.

7. Add the vermouth and sauté until the wine has nearly evaporated. Add the crushed tomatoes and simmer the mixture for twenty minutes, uncovered. Serve warm.

## Oyster Sausage

*Although you could use canned oysters in this recipe, in this case, it really is better to use the fresh variety.*

4 feet small (1½-inch diameter) hog casings
2 pounds shucked oysters, drained, liquid reserved
1 clove garlic, finely minced
1 teaspoon coarsely ground black pepper
1 egg, beaten
¼ cup chopped parsley
2 cups fresh bread crumbs

1. Prepare the casings. (See Chapter 4.)

2. Put the oysters in the bowl of a food processor and process until they are coarsely chopped.

3. Add the remaining ingredients and process until well blended. Add enough of the reserved oyster liquor to the mixture to make it form a stiff paste.

4. Stuff the mixture into the casings and twist off into three- to four-inch links.

# Chapter 10

# Sausage From Game Meats

I t is probably safe to say that the vast majority of people alive today in the civilized world have never tasted even some of the many species of wild game available to the hunter. In fact, one need not even be a hunter to sample some of nature's delicacies since many species of game are raised on licensed ranches and preserves, and their meat is available for sale to restaurants, butcher shops, and the general public. The fact that the corner grocery stocks only domestic fowl and red meat should not deter one from searching out the various game meats that are available. Check with your local butcher, the classified ads in many cooking magazines, and the appendix at the back of this book.

# Some General Thoughts About Game Cookery

Historically, game cookery is indigenous to the American culinary landscape. Our forefathers could not have survived had they not hunted for their food. They would not have flourished had they not found palatable and interesting ways of preparing the food they caught.

Many people today would probably starve if they had to rely on themselves to track, kill, dress, and prepare their own meat. Although hunters take pride in their skills and prowess, the fact of the matter is that most people would just as soon cook whatever they find in the meatcase of the corner grocery than bother with searching out more exotic meats.

Although we have gotten away from the need for finding our own sources of animal protein (and it is probably for the best that we have), a new dish, a different taste, or a unique recipe is always welcome to stave off the boredom that can ensue from eating the same old things, day after day, week after week. If you are interested in the challenge and excitement of trying something different, here are a few basic rules about cooking with game that have long since been forgotten (or indeed were probably never learned) by most modern cooks.

## Young is tender, old is tougher.

This adage is true whether we are talking about Ol' Bessie or about the bear you bagged yesterday. Certainly steaks, chops, and roasts are most people's first choices. But an animal has a fixed number of those choice parts. And the older the animal, the smaller the number. The fact of the matter is, if you are lucky enough to hunt down a trophy-sized specimen, then you will probably find yourself with more sausage meat than rib roast. A corollary to this rule is that the older the meat, the more developed the flavor. In other words, game does get gamier with age.

## The best dressed game is the best tasting game.

We're not talking Easter bonnets here. If you hunt for your own meat, be sure to field dress it properly. The size and species of the animal, as well as weather conditions, all play a role in determining the proper procedures to follow. If you are inexperienced or unsure about the right way to go about it, be sure to consult one of the many books and magazines that deal with hunting and preparing game.

## The essence is in the fat.

In big game, especially, the strongest flavor is found in the fat of the animal. Unless you really relish the strongest of gamy flavors, it is best to trim the fat from the game animal and replace it in a recipe with pork or beef fat which tend to be very mild.

## Some wild game animals bring home more than the bacon.

Bear and boar, just like domestic pork, can be carriers of trichinosis. **When cooking this meat it must be treated like pork.** (See Chapter 6.)

## By the tail hangs a tale.

The tale being that most game animals improve with aging, that is hanging. Just as domestic beef is aged, or "hung," so, too, must game be aged to improve flavor, texture, and tenderness. Again, if in doubt about proper procedures, check with a reliable source on game handling and cookery.

# Game Meat Characteristics

Every species' meat has its own very distinct characteristics. Most people could probably tell the difference between chicken and beef, even if they were blindfolded; not necessarily so much by the taste (which can be deceptive) as by the texture. "Mouth feel," the term food scientists use to describe how the texture of something feels in the mouth, is a reliable indicator of whether something we are chewing on is familiar or strange.

Although food scientists have their own vocabulary when it comes to what something tastes like, the fact of the matter is that most people would be hard put to describe what chicken tastes like, or what the taste difference is between a freshly caught brook trout and one that has languished three months in a freezer. We *know* the difference when we taste it, but just try to describe it to someone who has never tasted it. That's the problem one runs into when trying to describe what rabbit or elk or pheasant taste like to someone who has never partaken of them.

The following chart is a rough guide to what some of the more common game species taste like. It is a good place to start if you are unfamiliar with a particular species. It could also serve as a starting point when trying to decide what herbs and spices might go well with a particular meat.

| Game | Characteristics |
| --- | --- |
| Bear | Lean, dark meat. |
| Bison | Very similar to beef but some leaner. |
| Boar | Very much like pork but with a richer flavor. |
| Dove | Similar to the dark meat of chicken, tender and rich in flavor. |
| Duck | Dark, tender meat, very rich in flavor. |
| Elk | Dark meat similar to beef. |
| Goose | Dark, lean meat, very flavorful. |
| Moose | Similar to beef, but darker and richer in flavor. |
| Opossum | Similar to pork but with a distinctive gamy flavor. |
| Rabbit (cottontail) | Similar to chicken, light meat. |
| Squirrel | Pink, sweet meat. |
| Turkey | Lean, dark meat, very rich in flavor. |
| Venison (Whitetail deer) | Similar to beef but with more flavor. |
| Woodchuck | Rich, red flesh with a distinctive gamy favor. |

# Game Sausages

## Bear Sausage

*Chances are if you bag a bear, you are going to have to triple or quadruple this recipe, but this will give you a good idea of what kind of seasonings go well with bear meat.*

5 feet medium (2-inch diameter) hog casings
4 pounds bear meat trimmed of all fat, cubed*
1 pound pork fat, cubed*
2½ teaspoons salt
2 teaspoons freshly ground black pepper
1 teaspoon celery seed
½ teaspoon dried thyme leaves
½ teaspoon dried savory
½ cup dry red wine

1. Prepare the casings. (See Chapter 4.)
2. Mix the cubes of meat and fat together with the remaining ingredients.
3. Grind through the coarse disk.
4. Grind through the fine disk, stuff into casings, tie off into three-inch links and refrigerate to age for two days. Cook as for fresh pork sausage.

## Bison Bologna

*This isn't a true bologna like the one that you are accustomed to seeing in the deli case, but it has a richer flavor and a fine texture.*

5 feet medium (2-inch diameter) hog casings
4 pounds bison (buffalo) meat, with fat, cubed
1 pound beef fat, cubed
2 teaspoons salt
2 cloves garlic, finely minced
2 teaspoons finely chopped shallots
½ teaspoon cayenne pepper
2 teaspoons sweet paprika

1. Prepare the casings. (See Chapter 4.)
2. Grind the meat and fat together through the coarse disk.
3. Add the remaining ingredients and mix well.
4. Grind the mixture through the fine disk twice.
5. Stuff into casings, tie off into three- or four-inch links and cook as for any fresh sausage.

*Prepare bear or boar according to the instructions in Chapter 6 to assure that it is trichinosis free.

# Italian-Style Boar Sausage

*If you don't have access to boar meat, here is a trick you can use to make ordinary pork taste almost like the real thing.*

5 pounds fresh ham (not cured or smoked), boned and skinned, with fat
4 cups (or enough to cover) ruby port wine
1 tablespoon whole black pepper corns
1 tablespoon whole juniper berries
3 bay leaves
3—4 sprigs fresh thyme
3—4 whole fresh sage leaves

5 feet medium (2-inch diameter) hog casings
4 pounds boar, cubed*
1 pound pork fat, cubed*
OR
5 pounds fresh pork ham prepared according to the preceeding recipe, cubed
2½ teaspoons salt
2 teaspoons black pepper
2 teaspoons crushed fennel seed
Crushed red peppers to taste, optional

Lay the fresh ham out flat in a roasting pan just large enough to accommodate it. Pour the remaining ingredients over the meat and marinate for four days. Keep under refrigeration and turn the meat in the marinade at least once but preferably twice a day. At the end of the marinating time, pat the meat dry, removing any pieces of spices clinging to it and use as you would fresh boar meat. See the following recipe.

1. Prepare the casings. (See Chapter 4.)
2. Mix together the remaining ingredients.
3. Grind through the coarse disk and stuff into casings. Tie off into three- or four-inch links and prepare as for regular Italian sausage.

---

*Prepare bear or boar according to the instructions in Chapter 6 to assure that it is trichinosis free.

## Dove Links

*This is more of a novelty sausage than one you can actually sink your teeth into since the meat available on a single dove is less than a quarter pound. Consequently, if you make this sausage you might plan on it being simply an hors d'oeuvre item.*

1 pound fresh dove meat
   scraped from 8 to 10 doves
½ teaspoon salt
¼ teaspoon finely ground
   black pepper
¼ teaspoon ground thyme
¼ teaspoon ground sage
½ teaspoon finely ground
   ginger

1. Chill the meat in the freezer for fifteen minutes.
2. Grind the meat through the fine disk.
3. Mix the meat with the remaining ingredients and grind again through the fine disk.
4. Wet your hands with cold water, and taking about a tablespoon of meat at a time, form little "links" of sausage.
5. Refrigerate the links until firm, about thirty minutes and sauté in vegetable oil until browned on all sides. Serve warm.

## Duck Dogs

*This recipe is intended for the wild variety of duck and not the domesticated grocery store variety which would not stand up to the seasonings used here.*

*The larger species of wild ducks will yield approximately three-quarters of a pound of meat. Plan on about four ducks if you wish to make enough duck dogs to serve as an entrée.*

2–3 feet small (1½-inch
   diameter) hog or sheep
   casings
2 pounds fresh duck meat
2 tablespoons finely chopped
   fresh chives
2 cloves garlic, finely chopped
1 teaspoon ground coriander
   seed
¼ teaspoon ground mace
½ teaspoon finely ground white
   pepper
1 teaspoon sweet paprika
1 egg white

1. Prepare the casings. (See Chapter 4.)
2. Mix the remaining ingredients with the duck meat and refrigerate for thirty minutes.
3. Grind the mixture through the fine disk. Refrigerate to firm, about thirty minutes.
4. Stuff the meat into casings and tie off into four-inch links.
5. Bring a large pot of water to a boil, add the links, reduce heat, and simmer for thirty minutes. The sausages may be eaten after simmering, or they may be refrigerated and either served cold later or browned in a little oil and served warm.

## Elk Sausage

*Elk is an assertive meat and you need the seasonings to stand up to it. For five pounds of sausage:*

5 feet medium (2-inch diameter) hog casings
4 pounds elk meat, trimmed and cubed
1 pound beef fat
2½ teaspoons salt
2 teaspoons coarsely ground black pepper
2 teaspoons cayenne pepper
2 cloves garlic, finely chopped
1 teaspoon crushed anise seed
¼ cup dry red wine

1. Prepare the casings. (See Chapter 4.)
2. Grind the meat and fat together through the coarse disk.
3. Mix the remaining ingredients together with the meat.
4. Stuff the mixture into the casings and twist off into four-inch links. This is an assertive sausage and is best roasted or grilled.

## Goose-Neck Sausages

*Here is a novel way of stuffing sausage. Plan on about three pounds of usable meat from a large wild goose.*

2 pounds (about ten) chicken necks
3 pounds, approximately, fresh goose
½ teaspoon thyme
½ teaspoon sage
½ teaspoon marjoram
¼ teaspoon allspice
1 teaspoon salt
½ teaspoon finely ground white pepper
1 tablespoon vegetable oil

1. Carefully, so as not to tear them, remove the skin from the chicken necks. Use the necks for another purpose. (They make an excellent addition to the stock pot).
2. Mix the goose meat with the remaining ingredients.
3. Grind this mixture through the fine disk.
4. Sauté the mixture in a large skillet until the meat loses its raw look, about ten minutes. Allow to cool.
5. Tie one end of each of the chicken neck skins with kitchen twine. Stuff the skins with the goose mixture and tie off the other end. Bake for forty-five minutes in a preheated 375° F oven, until the skins are crispy. Serve warm.

## Moose Sausage

*If you like venision, you will probably like moose meat. It is very beefy—beefier than beef—with a rich flavor and a dark color. These sausages are assertively spiced to stand up to the rich flavor of the meat. Use the fat attached to the meat or trim it away and substitute an equal amount of beef fat.*

5 feet medium (2-inch diameter) hog casings
5 pounds moose with fat or 4 pounds meat and an equal amount of beef fat, cubed
2 teaspoons salt
2 teaspoons coarsely ground black pepper
2 cloves garlic, finely minced
¼ cup onion, finely minced
½ cup sweet red pepper, finely minced
1 teaspoon crushed red pepper

1. Prepare the casings. (See Chapter 4.)
2. Mix together the remaining ingredients.
3. Grind the mixture through the coarse disk and stuff into casings. Twist off into four-inch links and allow sausage to "cure" in the refrigerator for two days before cooking.

## Opossum Sausage

*There is no middle ground when it comes to opossum: you either like it or you don't. 'Posum, as it is usually referred to, can be very gamy—a quality one either relishes or abhors.*

5 feet medium (2-inch diameter) hog casings
4 pounds opossum, trimmed of all fat, cubed
1 pound pork fat, cubed*
2 teaspoons salt
2 teaspoons freshly ground white pepper
1 teaspoon hot pepper sauce, preferably Tabasco
1 teaspoon crushed cumin
1 teaspoon oregano
2 teaspoons sweet paprika

1. Prepare the casings. (See Chapter 4.)
2. Mix together the remaining ingredients.
3. Grind the mixture through the coarse blade and stuff into casings. Twist off into three- or four-inch links. Cook by sautéing in vegetable oil until well browned.

*See Chapter 6, page 44.

## Rabbit Sausage

*Although this recipe is specifically tailored to wild cotton-tail rabbit, you could substitute the domestic rabbit found in your grocer's meatcase. The flavor of the meat will be somewhat milder. In any case, the meat is very lean.*

3 feet small (1½-inch diameter)
   hog or sheep casings
3 pounds rabbit, cubed
1 teaspoon salt
½ teaspoon freshly ground
   white pepper
½ teaspoon freshly ground
   black pepper
½ teaspoon thyme
½ teaspoon freshly grated
   ginger
2 tablespoons chopped fresh
   chives
2 tablespoons chopped fresh
   parsley

1. Prepare the casings. (See Chapter 4.)
2. Mix the remaining ingredients.
3. Grind the mixture through the small disk and stuff into casings. Twist off into three-inch links. Pan fry in vegetable oil.

## Squirrel Sausage

*Because of the amount of meat found on a single squirrel, sweet and tasty though it may be, this sausage is another novelty sausage because of the amount one would be likely to make at one time.*

2 feet small (1-inch diameter)
   sheep casings
2 pounds squirrel meat
1 teaspoon salt
½ teaspoon freshly ground
   white pepper
2 tablespoons toasted pine nuts
⅛ teaspoon mace
⅛ teaspoon cardamom
⅛ teaspoon allspice

1. Prepare the casings. (See Chapter 4.)
2. Grind the squirrel meat through the fine disk.
3. Mix the meat with the remaining ingredients.
4. Grind the mixture through the fine disk and stuff into casings. Twist off into two-inch links, resembling "cocktail franks." Cook by steaming or simmering for about thirty minutes. Serve warm or cold.

## Wild Turkey Sausage

*This recipe is specifically geared to the use of wild turkey and not the domestic variety. The difference in the flavor of the two meats is as great as the difference in the two species' native intelligence.*

5 feet small (1½-inch diameter) hog or sheep casings
4 pounds wild turkey meat
2 teaspoons salt
1 teaspoon freshly ground white pepper
1 teaspoon celery seed
½ teaspoon powdered bay leaf
2 teaspoons lemon zest
2 tablespoons chopped fresh parsley
⅛ teaspoon ground cloves
¼ cup Wild Turkey Bourbon

1. Prepare the casings. (See Chapter 4.)
2. Mix the remaining ingredients.
3. Grind the mixture through the fine disk and stuff into casings. Twist off into three-inch links. Cook by sautéing in vegetable oil over medium heat until nicely browned and cooked through.

## Woodchuck Sausage

*Just like 'posum, woodchuck is another case of "I'm just wild about Woody," or you're not. If you find a big ol' 'chuck ravaging your sweet corn, however, you might be tempted to try this recipe.*

5 feet medium (2-inch diameter) hog casings
5 pounds woodchuck cubed
2 teaspoons salt
2 teaspoons freshly ground black pepper
2 cloves garlic, finely minced
½ cup onion, finely chopped
1 teaspoon dried rosemary, crushed
½ teaspoon sage
½ teaspoon thyme
2 tablespoons chopped parsley

1. Prepare the casings. (See Chapter 4.)
2. Mix together the remaining ingredients.
3. Grind the mixture through the coarse disk and then the fine disks and stuff into casings. Twist off into three-inch links. Cook by sautéing in vegetable oil.

## Venison Sausage

*The term venison actually refers to all members of the deer family, including elk, moose, and caribou. For simplicity's sake, however, when we say venison here, we mean the meat of the common Whitetail deer.*

5 feet medium (2-inch diameter) hog casings
5 pounds cubed, pre-frozen venison*
3 pounds lean pre-frozen or certified pork*
2 pounds pork fat, cubed*
5 tablespoons salt
1 teaspoon thyme
2 teaspoons sugar
1 tablespoon finely ground black pepper
2 teaspoons garlic, finely minced
1 tablespoon paprika
1 teaspoon cayenne red pepper
1 cup brandy
½ teaspoon ascorbic acid
1 teaspoon saltpeter
A marinade consisting of the following ingredients:
½ cup red wine vinegar
½ cup red wine
2 teaspoons salt
1 small onion, sliced
½ cup thinly sliced carrot
1 clove garlic, finely minced
1 bay leaf
¼ cup chopped heart of celery
1 tablespoon whole black peppercorns

1. After the pre-frozen venison has thawed, prepare the marinade and pour it over the cubes of meat. Marinate in the refrigerator for twenty-four hours.

2. Drain the venison, discard the marinade, and grind the meat through the fine disk.

3. Grind the pork and fat separately through the fine disk and mix with the venison.

4. Add the remaining ingredients and mix thoroughly. Place the sausage in the refrigerator overnight.

5. Prepare the casings. (See Chapter 4.)

6. Stuff the mixture into the casings and tie off into four- or five-inch links.

7. Hang the sausage to dry for forty-eight hours.

8. Cold smoke the sausage (70–90° F) for ten hours.

9. Hang again for at least two weeks before sampling.

*See Chapter 6, page 44.

# Chapter 11

# Putting It All Together

Every summer our area becomes a showcase for ethnic cuisines. The Italians have their field (or feast) days of Saint Anthony; the Czechs, Slavs, Russians, Ukrainians, Poles, and Greeks each have their own weekend of feasting, partying, dancing, and gaming—not to mention imbibing. For one weekend a year, a public picnic area, a grassy field or a church parking lot becomes Little Italy, Little Prague or Little any one of many varied cultures and cuisines. The beer and wine flow freely. The music lasts until the wee hours of the morning. Always the public is invited. And always—without reservation—the charcoal fires in the makeshift brick and cinderblock pits are kept burning to accommodate the barbecued chickens, steaks, and sausages that keep the revelers reveling, holding hunger at bay and, for three days at least, making life's problems blow away on the wood smoke-scented breeze. A soft summer's night, music, dancing, ice cold beer trickling down your throat, a hot sausage spurting juice on the first bite: it may not be heaven, but it sure comes close!

Good times and good food belong to the same brotherhood. Regardless of the nationality, people parade the best of their cuisine during times of partying and feasting. And one ingredient seems to play an important part in everyone of them: the sausage. Sausage and good times go together like wine and cheese, like the Fourth of July and fireworks. Sausage is a fun food. I told you in the beginning of this book that sausage is fun to make and, I trust, I've convinced you of that. Now I want to show you that making sausage is not merely intrinsically satisfying, but also is a very pleasant means to a most gratifying end. Whether it is served as an *hors d'oeuvre,* for breakfast, or as the main part of a meal, sausage forever reminds us of how versatile, simple to prepare, and how satisfying it can make a meal.

The recipes in this chapter are family favorites. They range from the most simple to quite extravagant and elaborate. They all have two things in common: they all rely on some kind of sausage as an integral ingredient and they are all delicious. As I said earlier about making sausage—make these recipes your own. Try them my way first and then experiment to suit your and your family's tastes. Consider them my gift to you: your reward for being a *wurstmacher*!

# Hors D'Oeuvres

The French call them *hors d'oeuvres,* the Italians *antipasto* and Americans are most apt to refer to them as appetizers or munchies. In our house we call them *oover doovers*, which no doubt makes Charles de Gaulle roll over in his grave, but it nevertheless gets the message across. Next to the cracker, one of the most frequently used ingredients in many before meal treats is some kind of sausage. This attests to sausage's versatility and indicates that it can be prepared alone or in conjunction with other ingredients which tempt the palate without overtaxing the cook's time or energies.

## Braunschweiger Meatballs

*This is an easy, quick to prepare party dish which can be prepared a day or two ahead and refrigerated until needed.*

½ pound homemade braunschweiger sausage
2 teaspoons freshly grated onion
½ teaspoon garlic, finely minced
Dash of hot pepper sauce
Salt to taste
Freshly ground black pepper to taste
2 tablespoons chopped fresh parsley
Toothpicks

1. Mash the braunschweiger with a fork and add the onion, garlic, hot pepper sauce, salt, and pepper. Mix through.

2. Form the mixture into twenty- or twenty-five little meatballs and roll each one in the parsley to coat.

3. Insert a toothpick into each ball and chill before serving. Serves 4 to 6.

# Broiled Sausage and Mozzarella
# Mini-Submarine Sandwich

*A whole sandwich is more than enough for a meal for one person, but if you cut it into six or eight pieces you will have a tasty appetizer.*

*First of all, a note about the term "submarine sandwich." It seems to depend on what part of the country you are from as to what you call a long sandwich. One common name is the "Dagwood" after the cartoon strip character by the same name who has been known to raid the refrigerator in the wee hours of the morning and pile almost anything high on a bun. "Grinder" is another term frequently employed and its etymology is elusive. One might guess that it derives from the fact that you really have to "grind down" to consume a sandwich of this size and scope. Another common name for a sandwich of this description is "hoagie." Your guess is as good as mine as to where that name comes from. "Hero" is another popular term and I presume that the term relates to the fact that it is a sandwich made for a hero, or perhaps you might be considered a hero if you can get the whole thing down.*

*At any rate, one of the most common names for a long sandwich is "submarine"—no doubt because it is shaped like one. No matter where you live or what you call it, a sub is a Dagwood is a grinder is a hero is a sub.*

**1 submarine sandwich roll about twelve inches long (or use a loaf of French bread cut to size)**

**¾ pound hot or sweet Italian-style sausage***

**4 ounces shredded mozzarella cheese**

1. Parboil the sausage over medium heat for about twenty minutes with enough water to barely cover the bottom of a skillet. Increase the heat and brown the sausage lightly, about five minutes.

2. Cut the sausage lengthwise almost, but not quite all the way through and spread it out flat.

3. Cut the sub roll in the same manner as the sausage and place the sausage in the center of the roll.

4. Sprinkle the mozzarella cheese evenly over the sausage and place the sub, open side up, in a preheated broiler for two minutes or just until the cheese is melted. Remove from the broiler, close the sandwich, and cut into serving pieces while still warm.

Serves 8 as an appetizer.

---

*If you know that you are going to be making this recipe when you are making sausage, simply make the links the length of the sub roll and everything will fit very nicely.

# Calzone

*Calzone (pronounced cäl zŏ nēē) are an Italian invention which could be a main dish, a hearty snack, or a delicious appetizer. As appetizers, they can be quite filling so they are best served when a relatively light meal is to follow. Serve them piping hot, but warn your guests to be careful not to burn their mouths on the bubbling cheese inside.*

*The dough for calzone is a standard Neopolitan pizza dough. (You could also substitute a frozen bread or pizza dough—just thaw according to package directions.)*

**For the dough:**

1 package (¼ ounce) active
   dry yeast
¾ cup plus ½ cup warm water
Salt to taste
3 cups flour
1 tablespoon olive oil

**For the filling:**

1 pound bulk Italian-style
   sweet sausage
1 small onion, diced
½ pound pepperoni, salami or
   soppresatta or a combination
   of these cut into ¼ inch
   cubes
1 tablespoon chopped fresh
   Italian parsley

**Optional:**

Chopped pitted black olives
Mashed anchovies
Capers
Chopped red, green or yellow
   peppers
Crushed red pepper
2 tablespoons olive oil
2 cups shredded mozzarella
   cheese (may be part skim)
Salt and freshly ground black
   pepper to taste

1. Make the dough as follows: Mix the packet of yeast into ¾ cup of warm water and allow to sit for fifteen minutes until bubbles form; add salt to flour if desired (a little salt helps improve the texture of the dough); gradually add the yeast and water and one tablespoon oil; work on a floured surface, gradually add the half cup of water and knead the dough for about ten minutes. Place the dough in a lightly greased bowl, cover, put it in a warm place and let it double in size.

2. Prepare the filling: crumble the sausage in a skillet and sauté it until it loses its pink color, about five or ten minutes. Remove the sausage with a slotted spoon to a mixing bowl and add the chopped onion to the pan with the sausage drippings. Sauté the onion until it is translucent, about five minutes. Drain the onion and add it to the sausage. Mix in the cubed sausage meat, parsley, and any optional ingredients to taste, salt, and pepper.

3. Remove the dough from the bowl and place it on a floured work surface. Divide it into four or eight equal portions. Roll each portion out so that the dough is about an eighth of an inch thick.

4. Brush each circle with the olive oil, leaving a one-inch border free.

5. Divide the sausage mixture equally among the circles of dough, placing it to one side of center. Sprinkle an equal amount of mozzarella on each.

6. Carefully fold each piece of dough over to form a semi-circle and press to seal the edges.

7. Brush the tops of the calzone with olive oil and place them on a lightly greased cookie sheet.

8. Bake the calzone in a preheated 450° F oven for twenty-five minutes or until they are golden brown. Serve piping hot.

Serves 4 to 8.

## Breadless Salami Sandwich

*The Earl of Sandwich would ask where the bread is in this sandwich, but since he's not around to ask, just make it and enjoy it.*

½ pound thinly sliced home-
made hard salami
Dijon-style mustard
Chopped parsley
Carrots cut into julienne strips
Celery cut into julienne strips

Spread each slice of salami with a thin coating of mustard, sprinkle the parsley on each slice, and place several strips of carrot and celery on each. Roll up and arrange on a platter and serve.

Serves 6 to 8 depending on how thinly the salami is sliced.


## Chorizo Tostadas

*This recipe is a three-alarmer—or four—depending on how hot you make your chorizos. A tostada is a tortilla which is crisp-fried and covered with all sorts of yummy things.*

*Either buy commercially prepared tortillas or make the following recipe:*

3 cups yellow corn meal
2 cups sifted flour
2 teaspoons salt, or to taste
4 tablespoons vegetable shortening
Warm water

1. Mix the cornmeal and salt with the flour in a bowl.
2. Cut in the shortening in small pieces as you would if you were making a pie crust.
3. Begin adding water slowly, mixing it thoroughly. You will probably need about one cup to make a workable dough.
4. Knead the dough for five minutes and then divide it into small pieces. Roll each piece into a ball. They should be about the size of golf balls.
5. Flatten each ball and roll it into a circle.
6. Cook each circle in an ungreased frying pan for about two minutes on each side. A non-stick skillet works beautifully.
7. When all the tortillas are cooked, add enough vegetable oil to the skillet to cover the bottom and fry each tortilla until it is crisp and golden.

**To assemble the tostadas you will need:**

1 pound fresh chorizos
removed from the casing
and crumbled
¼ cup chopped jalapeño
peppers, or to taste
8 ounces shredded Monterey
Jack or Cheddar cheese

1. Sauté the sausage until it is lightly browned. Drain well.
2. Place an equal amount of sausage, jalapeños and cheese on each tortilla. Place them under a preheated broiler for a minute or two, or just until the cheese melts.

Makes about 15 to 20 tostadas, enough for 8 to 10 as an appetizer.

# Garlic Salami Squares

*The French would call these appetizers* canapés *meaning that they are bite-sized* hors d'oeuvres *on a piece of bread.*

½ cup *aioli* (garlic mayonnaise —See Step 1)
½ pound homemade hard salami
3 hard-boiled eggs
1 teaspoon Pernod liqueur
Chopped parsley
Pimiento strips
Thinly sliced bread

1. Make the *aioli* as follows: mash ten cloves of garlic (peeled) with a mortar and pestle or in a food processor. In a mixing bowl, scramble two egg yolks, add the garlic, salt to taste, the juice of one lemon, and a pinch of freshly ground white pepper. Mix very well. While vigorously beating with a wire whisk or with the food processor running, *slowly* dribble one and one-half cups of olive oil into the bowl. Reserve one-half cup of this *aioli* for the Garlic Salami Squares and refrigerate the rest.

2. Cut the crust from several slices of thinly sliced bread. Divide each slice into four squares. Toast the slices until they are golden brown.

3. Cube the salami and cut it through the fine disk of a food grinder.

4. Chop the hard-boiled eggs finely and combine with the salami, Pernod and half a cup of *aioli*. Mix well.

5. Spread each slice of toast with some of the salami mixture, sprinkle with parsley and criss-cross with pimiento strips. *Voila! Bon appétit!*

Makes about twenty-four canapés or enough for 8 to 10 servings.

# Ghina's Cheese and Sausage Roll

*This recipe is the creation of a dear friend, Elnora Luizzi, who, in the finest Italian tradition, keeps a warm home open to family and friends where the food, wine, and conversation flow freely. Mrs. Luizzi's grandchildren call her Ghina and since she never bothered to title this recipe, I've taken the liberty of naming it for her.*

*Depending on the texture you like best use either the pizza dough recipe on page 98 or the pie crust dough below.*

1 pound sweet Italian-style sausage, removed from casing and crumbled
1 recipe pizza or pie crust dough
8 ounces mozzarella or Swiss cheese, grated
Olive oil

1. Crumble the sausage in a skillet and sauté over medium heat until lightly browned, about ten minutes. Remove the meat with a slotted spoon and set aside.

2. Roll out the dough into a rectangle about twelve by eighteen inches and about a quarter of an inch thick.

3. Brush the dough with olive oil leaving a one-inch border all around.

4. Spread the sausage evenly on the dough and top with the grated cheese.

5. Roll up the dough, jelly roll fashion, being careful to tuck in the ends and seal the edges.

6. Place the roll carefully on a cookie sheet, seam side down, and bake in a preheated 375° F oven for thirty to forty-five minutes or until the crust is crispy and golden.

7. Cool about twenty minutes and slice into half-inch thick serving pieces.

Serves 8 to 10.

## Optional Pie Crust Dough

2 cups sifted flour
1 teaspoon salt, or to taste
⅔ cup vegetable shortening
4—6 tablespoons ice water

1. Sift the flour and salt together in a large mixing bowl.
2. Blend in the shortening with a pastry blender.
3. Sprinkle in the ice water, a tablespoon at a time, mixing well, using only enough water to form the dough in a ball.

## Guacamole Dip with Chorizos

*Avocados are interesting even though their flesh is rather boring to taste. In combination with other things, however, they take on new life. The two most interesting things you can do with an avocado are (1) grow a tree from the pit and (2) make guacamole. Whether you decide to do either or both is up to you, but if you've never tried this Mexican dip, I urge you to do so.*

*Guacamole doesn't usually have meat in it, but this version is an excellent vehicle for showing off your home-made chorizos. You can tailor the recipe to either fresh or dried chorizos, depending upon what you have on hand.*

½ pound fresh or dried chorizos
1 ripe avocado
1 medium tomato, cored, peeled, seeded, and finely diced
2 cloves garlic, finely minced
½ cup mayonnaise
Dash hot pepper sauce
Salt and freshly ground black pepper to taste

1. If you are using fresh chorizos remove them from the casing and sauté them, breaking them up with a wooden spoon until they are done, about twenty minutes. If you are using dry chorizos, cut them into half-inch cubes and whirl them in the food processor until they are finely crumbled.

2. Peel the avocado and cut it in half to remove the pit. If you plan on saving the pit to grow an avocado tree, be careful not to cut through the pit's outer shell. Mash the avocado in a bowl, using the back of a fork or process in a food processor. Mash or process until you get a smooth puree.

3. Add the chopped tomato to the avocado and mix through.

4. Mix in the chorizo, garlic, mayonnaise, hot pepper sauce, salt, and pepper. Serve well chilled with corn chips.

Plenty of dip for 8 to 10 people.

# Hot Dog Wraparounds

*This is hardly a new idea as far as appetizers go, but try it with your homemade wieners and see if it doesn't make a whopping difference.*

1 pound homemade hot dogs
Swiss or Cheddar cheese
Bacon
Toothpicks

1. Cut the hot dogs lengthwise without cutting all the way through.
2. Cut the cheese into sticks and put one into each hot dog.
3. Wrap each hot dog with a slice of bacon and secure with a toothpick.
4. Broil until the cheese melts and the bacon is crisp. Cut into one-inch chunks and serve warm.
Serves 10 to 12 with about forty pieces.

# Liverwurst Munchies

*Romeo and Juliet . . . pussywillows and springtime . . . liverwurst and onions . . . and mayonnaise . . . need I say more? This is a classic combination, easy to prepare and delicious.*

½ pound homemade liverwurst
Mayonnaise
1 small Bermuda onion, sliced
   very thin
Stuffed green olives, sliced
Toasted rounds of French or
   Italian bread

1. Mash the liverwurst with just enough mayonnaise to moisten it slightly.
2. Place a thin slice of onion on each toast round and spread the liverwurst over the onion.
3. Garnish with the sliced olives.
Serves 8 to 10.

# Pumpernickel Sausage and Cheese Squares

*Use any cured or dried sausage you have on hand, such as kielbasa or bologna, for this recipe.*

½ pound sliced sausage, cut
   into one-inch squares
½ pound sliced Swiss,
   provolone, Muenster or
   mozzarella cheese, cut into
   one-inch squares
7 large pitted black or green
   stuffed olives, sliced
5 slices pumpernickel bread cut
   into two-inch squares

Arrange one slice of sausage, one slice of cheese, and one slice of olive on each bread square. Makes about twenty servings.
Serves 8 to 10.

## Marinated Antipasto Platter

*There are as many different combinations possible for this dish as there are recipes for spaghetti sauce. What is really nice about this recipe is that you can vary it every time you make it depending upon what you have on hand. In Italian, this particular dish is sometimes referred to as a "garden salad" because just about anything from the garden can be tossed into it.*

*Use this dish to show off your homemade salamis. The more variety, the better. I'll leave the exact quantities up to you. The only steadfast rule to follow is to be creative!*

**Salami (at least two different varieties) cut into half-inch cubes**
**Cheese—Asiago, Mozzarella, provolone, Scamorze, Swiss— any combination, cut into half-inch cubes**
**Celery, sliced**
**Carrots, sliced**
**Peppers, sweet red, green, yellow, and purple, cut into strips**
**Mushrooms, fresh buttons or slices**
**Cauliflower, broken into florets**
**Tomatoes, cherry or quartered medium**
**Green onions**
**Basil leaves, fresh, shredded**
**Oregano, one or two fresh sprigs, chopped**
**Olive oil**
**Lemon juice**
**Red wine vinegar**
**Salt to taste, if desired**
**Freshly ground black pepper**

In a mixing bowl large enough to hold all the ingredients, mix together the salamis and whatever vegetables you choose to use. Pour just enough olive oil in to coat the mixture lightly. Dribble in a small amount of lemon juice and red wine vinegar and mix through well. Add the basil and oregano, salt and pepper, and taste for seasoning. Refrigerate the mixture for about two hours before serving to allow the flavors to blend. Serve with a crusty French or Italian bread.

Serves any number depending upon quantity.

## Inside-Out Sausage Balls

*Here's a new variation on an old theme—the sausage is on the outside.*

**½ pound braunschweiger**
**Pimiento or almond stuffed olives**
**Pickled cocktail onions**
**Chopped parsley**

1. Mash the braunschweiger with a fork and then form balls around the individual olives and onions.
2. Roll each ball in the chopped parsley. Chill before serving.

Serves 10 to 12 as an appetizer.

# Mashed Potato Sausage Balls

*In this dish, the sausage is on the inside.*

1 pound bulk country-style
   sausage
2–3 cups mashed potatoes
2 eggs, well beaten
2 tablespoons water
1 cup dry bread crumbs
2 tablespoons grated Parmesan
   cheese
½ teaspoon basil
½ teaspoon oregano
1 tablespoon chopped fresh
   parsley
1 teaspoon finely ground white
   pepper
Dash of cayenne pepper

1. Form the sausage meat into small balls.
2. Coat each ball with mashed potatoes. It will be easier if the potatoes are slightly stiff.
3. Make a wash with the eggs and water.
4. Combine the bread crumbs with the remaining ingredients.
5. Dip each ball into the egg wash and then gently roll it in the seasoned bread crumbs. Place the balls on a baking sheet and let them rest for an hour or so to allow the crumb coating to set.
6. Deep fat fry the balls at 375° F until they are golden. Serve hot.

Serves 8 to 10.

# Piglets in a Blanket

*What look like miniature bread loaves on the outside, hide a real treat on the inside.*

1 pound sweet or hot Italian-
   style sausage or fresh chorizos
1 recipe pizza dough (see page
   98)

1. Parboil the sausages in just enough water to cover the bottom of a skillet until they are just cooked through, about twenty-five minutes, over medium heat. Drain off the liquid and brown the sausages lightly.
2. Divide the pizza dough into as many equal pieces as you have sausage links. Roll out each piece into a square.
3. Place a sausage on one end of each square and roll up the dough. Press to seal the edges.
4. Place each piglet on a greased cookie sheet and bake in a preheated 375° F oven for about twenty minutes or until the dough is golden brown. Serve warm.

Makes 4 to 6 piglets which may serve up to 6 to 8 people when sliced.

## Pizza Rustica

*Pizza rustica is a misnomer in a sense because this dish is anything but rustic. It requires careful attention to detail if you want it to be as pleasing to the eye as it is to the palate. Plan on eight servings for an antipasto or six servings as the main course at a luncheon. With a dry, well chilled white wine and a tossed green salad, this dish could be a complete meal.*

1 recipe pie crust dough (see page 101)
¼ pound sweet Italian-style sausage removed from the casing
2 tablespoons olive oil
1 small onion, chopped
2 cloves garlic, minced
¼ cup chopped red and green sweet peppers
¼ cup pepperoni, diced
¼ cup hard salami, diced
8 ounces mozzarella, shredded
¼ cup grated Parmesan cheese
¼ cup spaghetti sauce
1 tablespoon black olives, pitted and chopped
Salt to taste
Freshly ground black pepper

1. Prepare the pie crust dough and divide it in half. Roll out one piece and place it in a deep dish nine-inch pie plate. Roll out the other half of the dough and reserve it for the top crust.

2. Crumble the sausage in a skillet and add the olive oil. Sauté until the meat loses its pink color. Remove it with a slotted spoon and set it aside.

3. Drain off all but one tablespoon of oil and sauté the onion, garlic, and chopped peppers until they are crisp-tender. Remove them with a slotted spoon and discard the oil.

4. Mix together the sausage, pepperoni, salami, onions, peppers, and chopped olives. Add salt and pepper to taste.

5. Spread a thin layer of mozzarella on the bottom crust. Add about a third of the meat mixture and spread it evenly over the cheese. Dot with about a third of the spaghetti sauce and then sprinkle on a third of the Parmesan cheese. Repeat the layering process, ending with a layer of mozzarella.

6. Place the top crust over the filling and press with a fork to seal the edges.

7. Brush the top crust with cold water and bake in a preheated 350° F oven for forty-five minutes or until the top is golden.

Serves 6 to 8.

## Salami Asparagus Spears

*This is a great way to announce the arrival of spring. Your salami has been aging all winter while your garden was asleep. When those first tender shoots of asparagus poke their heads through the chilly soil, you know that spring is just around the corner.*

Asparagus spears, small
½ pound sliced hard salami
*Aioli* (see recipe page 100)

1. Wash and trim the asparagus under cold running water. Cut off enough of the bottom end of each spear so that all the spears are uniform in length and about as long as a slice of salami is wide.

2. Spread a teaspoon of *aioli* on each slice of salami.

3. Place an asparagus spear on each slice and roll it up. Serve well chilled.

Serves 8 to 10.

# Salami Log

*This appetizer is just the thing to impress guests with both your sausage making skills and with your flare for the creative.*

½ pound thinly sliced hard salami

1 3-ounce package cream cheese at room temperature

1 teaspoon chopped fresh chives

1 teaspoon chopped fresh parsley

1 teaspoon chopped pickled capers

1 teaspoon chopped sweet gherkin

1. Spread the cream cheese on the slices of salami.
2. Sprinkle the remaining ingredients evenly over all the slices.
3. Roll up the first slice of salami, but before it is completely rolled, overlap the end by about one inch on the next slice of salami and continue to roll. Repeat until you have a large roll.
4. Refrigerate for several hours to chill thoroughly and then cut into quarter-inch slices with a very sharp knife. Arrange on a platter and serve cold.

Serves 6 to 8.

# Salami Rollups

*You could substitute any large cured sausage for the salami in this recipe.*

½ pound thinly sliced hard salami or other cured sausage

1 pint sour cream (or substitute plain low-fat yogurt)

1 envelope dry instant onion soup mix

1 tablespoon dry sherry

1 tablespoon chopped fresh parsley

1. In a mixing bowl combine the sour cream or yogurt, soup mix, sherry, and parsley. Mix well.
2. Place about a tablespoon of this mixture on each slice of sausage towards one side. Roll up each slice and place it on a platter with the seam side down. Serve well chilled.

Serves 6 to 8.

# Sausage-Stuffed Artichokes

*I've tried for many years without success to grow my own artichokes from seed. They always come up, look good for a while, and then turn their best to the sky and go to vegetable heaven. Consequently, when my grocer gets in some real beauties, I grab a whole bunch and rush home with them.*

*There are lots of things you can do with artichokes. If you are lucky enough to grow your own, you can let some of them mature to form large beautiful flowers. Or, you can pick them when they are still young and tender (you actually eat the unopened flower bud of the plant) and boil them in salted water with some bay leaf, garlic and lemon wedges. Pull off the leaves (petals), dip them in drawn butter, and scrape off the succulent flesh between your teeth.*

*For variety, however, an artichoke is eminently stuffable.*

**4 large artichokes**
**4 bay leaves**
**4 cloves garlic, crushed**
**1 lemon, quartered**
**1 pound country-style bulk sausage or sweet Italian-style sausage removed from the casing**
**¼ cup minced onion**
**¼ cup Parmesan cheese**
**½ cup bread crumbs**
**1 egg, well beaten**
**½ cup dry white wine**
**1 teaspoon thyme**
**1 tablespoon chopped capers**
**Pinch of cayenne pepper**
**Salt to taste, if desired**
**Freshly ground black pepper**
**½ cup lemon juice**
**¼ cup olive oil**
**2 cloves garlic, finely minced**

1. Prepare the artichokes. Cut off the stem, leaving a flat base. Reserve the stems. Remove any bruised outer leaves. Cut about one inch off the top of each artichoke with a sharp knife. With a pair of kitchen scissors, snip off the tip of each outer leaf.

2. Place the artichokes in a pot of boiling water along with the bay leaves, four crushed cloves of garlic, and the quartered lemon. Add the stems to the pot and cook, covered, for about half an hour. Remove and cool.

3. While the artichokes are cooking, sauté the sausage in a skillet just until it loses its pink color. Remove with a slotted spoon and set aside.

4. In the sausage drippings, sauté the minced onion until it is translucent, about ten minutes.

5. In a bowl, mix the sausage, onion, Parmesan cheese, bread crumbs, egg, wine, thyme, capers, cayenne, salt, and pepper. When they are cooked, the artichoke stems should be chopped finely.

6. When the artichokes are cooked and cool enough to handle, pull back the leaves and remove the inner choke.

7. Fill the center of each artichoke with equal amounts of stuffing. If you have enough stuffing, place some between the large leaves at the base.

8. Place the stuffed artichokes in a baking pan and pour the lemon juice, mixed with the olive oil and minced garlic, over them. cover and bake in a preheated 350° F oven for about twenty minutes or until the base leaves are very tender. Serve hot with the pan juices for dipping.

Serves 4.

## Sausage-Stuffed Mushrooms

*This hors d'oeuvre is convenient. It looks sophisticated, as if it took a long time to prepare. A half an hour is plenty of time for anyone who knows his or her way around a kitchen to fix this dish. It may be refrigerated, then reheated just before guests arrive. To make this recipe work well, try to find mushrooms at least an inch and a half in diameter.*

18 large mushroom caps
2 tablespoons butter
¼ pound sweet Italian or country-style bulk sausage
2 tablespoons finely minced onions
2 tablespoons olive oil
¼ cup dry bread crumbs
2 tablespoons dry sherry
½ teaspoon oregano
1 tablespoon fresh parsley, chopped
1 clove garlic, very finely minced
Salt to taste, if desired
Freshly ground black pepper
¼ pound mozzarella, grated

1. Wash the mushrooms and remove the stems. Chop the stems finely and set aside.

2. Melt two tablespoons butter in a large skillet and gently sauté the mushroom caps for two to three minutes or until they are slightly golden but remove them before they are noticeably shrunken. Remove them with a slotted spoon and drain them on a paper towel.

3. Add the sausage and onions to the skillet and sauté for five minutes, until the meat loses its pink color and the onions are crisp-tender.

4. Add the two tablespoons of olive oil to the skillet along with the chopped mushroom stems and sauté another two minutes.

5. Remove from heat and add the bread crumbs, sherry, oregano, parsley, garlic, salt, and pepper and mix well. Add the mozzarella cheese and stir.

6. Place an equal amount of stuffing mixture in each cap.

7. Place the caps on a greased cookie sheet and put in a preheated broiler for one or two minutes or until the cheese bubbles. Serve hot or refrigerate and reheat when needed.

Serves 6 to 8.

## Skewered Sausage Squares

*This is a variation on the shish kebab theme. Any hard or semi-hard sausage works well in this recipe, so tailor it to what you have on hand or have a taste for.*

½ pound cured sausage cut into half-inch cubes
½ pound Swiss or mozzarella cheese cut into half-inch cubes
¼ cup unsalted butter or vegetable oil
1 teaspoon lemon juice
½ teaspon paprika
Dash of cayenne pepper
Toothpicks

1. Alternate cubes of sausage and cheese on the toothpicks. About two of each will probably fit perfectly.

2. Melt the butter or add the vegetable oil to a medium-sized skillet and add the lemon juice, paprika, and cayenne pepper.

3. Sauté the skewers briefly until the cheese gets soft but does not melt. Serve warm on a heated platter.

Serves 8 to 10.

## Snowball Liverwurst Pâté

Pâté de foie gras *is a famous (or infamous, if you look at it from the goose's point of view) French delicacy. In order to produce* pâté de foie gras, *the geese are put through the rather indelicate procedure of being force-fed. This operation continues, often to the point of suffocation, over a period of time necessary for their livers to become enlarged. Whether you are squeamish about what they do to their geese in France, or simply don't want to spend what it takes for this pricey product, you can still eat your pâté and have your goose, too: chicken livers and homemade liverwurst fill the bill nicely.*

4 ounces chicken livers
3 tablespoons butter
2 cloves garlic, minced
2 green onions with tops, minced
1 teaspoon basil
4 ounces liverwurst
1 tablespoon Drambuie (Scotch liqueur)
1 3-ounce package cream cheese
Salt to taste, if desired
Freshly ground black pepper
¼ cup chopped fresh parsley

1. Sauté the chicken livers in the butter in a skillet over medium heat for about fifteen minutes.
2. Add the garlic, onions, and basil and sauté a minute or two longer.
3. Dice the liverwurst and add it to the livers. Remove from heat.
4. Puree the mixture in a food processor, add the Drambuie, salt, and pepper and process until blended.
5. Lightly oil a small gelatin mold and pack the mixture into it firmly. Refrigerate for at least four hours.
6. Bring the cream cheese to room temperature and whip or beat it until it is smooth. (You may add an extra teaspoon of liqueur and a little finely minced garlic for added flavor.)
7. Unmold the pâté onto a serving dish and frost it with the cream cheese.
8. Gently press the chopped parsley into the cheese frosting. Serve chilled with bread or crackers.
Serves 8 to 10.

## Sweet and Sour Sausage Spears

*Homemade bologna, smoked kielbasa or summer sausage is perfect in this recipe.*

½ pound dry or semi-dry sausage, cut into half-inch cubes
Pineapple cubes
Pickled beets, cubed
Toothpicks

Arrange alternating pieces of meat, pineapple, and beets on toothpicks and serve well chilled.

**Note:** For an interesting variation, soak the assembled skewers in slightly sweet wine or your favorite liqueur overnight.
Serves 8 to 10.

## Sausage-Stuffed Tomatoes

*Choose small (but not cherry) tomatoes for this recipe, or it may be too filling for an appetizer.*

8 small tomatoes
½ pound bulk sausage
¼ cup chopped onion
¼ cup chopped sweet pepper
1 clove garlic, minced
1 egg, well beaten
Dry bread crumbs
Salt to taste, if desired
Freshly ground black pepper
Butter or olive oil

1. Cut a small slice off the stem end of each tomato and remove the seeds and pulp. Be careful not to puncture the tomato wall. Reserve the pulp.

2. Crumble the sausage in a skillet, and sauté over medium heat until lightly browned, about ten minutes. Remove the meat with a slotted spoon and set it aside.

3. Sauté the onions, pepper, and garlic in the sausage drippings until they are crisp-tender, about five minutes. Remove them with a slotted spoon.

4. Combine the sausage, onions, peppers, and garlic with an equal amount of bread crumbs, the egg, and about one half of the reserved pulp. Blend the mixture thoroughly.

5. Stuff the tomatoes with the sausage mixture and place on a greased cookie sheet. Dot each tomato with the butter or olive oil. Bake in a preheated 400° F oven for fifteen minutes or until the tops are browned.

Serves 8.

## Texas-Style Barbecue Dogs

*Here is another elegant way to serve the lowly hot dog.*

1 pound homemade hot dogs
2 tablespoons vegetable oil
1 16-ounce can tomato sauce
  (or use spaghetti sauce)
1 small onion, chopped
1 clove garlic, minced
¼ cup brown sugar
¼ cup cider vinegar
1 tablespoon Worchestershire
  sauce
1 teaspoon Tabasco sauce
¼ teaspoon celery seed
¼ teaspoon fenugreek
1 teaspoon dry mustard
1 teaspoon freshly ground
  white pepper
½ teaspoon finely ground coriander
Salt to taste, if desired

1. Cut the dogs into one-inch pieces and sauté in the oil until browned.

2. Combine the remaining ingredients and pour over the hot dogs. Simmer gently for about ten minutes. Serve in a chafing dish with toothpicks for skewers.

Serves 10 to 12.

# Thuringer Spears

*You can use any hard or semi-hard sausage for this recipe.*

½ pound Thuringer or other
    hard or semi-hard sausage,
    cubed
Pickled cocktail onions
Pitted black olives
1 tablespoon olive oil
1 teaspoon liquid from the
    pickled onions
½ teaspoon sugar

1. Alternate chunks of sausage with onions and olives on the toothpicks.
2. Combine the oil, pickling liquid, and sugar and mix well. Pour over the spears and serve.

Serves 6 to 8.

# Toasted Salami Skewers

*Assemble these* hors d'oeuvres *ahead of time and store them in the refrigerator. To serve, allow them to come to room temperature and pop them into the broiler or toaster oven just before company comes.*

4 slices thinly sliced hard
    salami
20 green stuffed olives
20 cocktail onions
Toothpicks
1 tablespoon olive oil
1 cup pineapple juice

1. Cut the salami into strips. You should get about five strips from each slice.
2. Assemble by pushing a toothpick through one end of a strip of salami. Skewer an olive and bring the salami over the skewer to cover one side of the olive. Skewer an onion and repeat the process with the salami so that the salami forms an "S" shape around the olives and onions.
3. Combine the olive oil and pineapple juice and brush on each skewer.
4. Toast lightly in a preheated broiler for about two minutes or until warmed through.

Serves 6 to 8.

## Turkey Sausage Strudel

*Make strudel dough according to your favorite recipe, or use ready made* phyllo *dough available in your grocer's freezer section.*

1 tablespoon vegetable oil
¾ pound fresh turkey sausage, removed from the casing
¼ cup finely minced onion
2 cloves garlic, finely minced
8 ounces fresh mushrooms, finely chopped
¼ cup fresh parsley, finely minced
2 ounces cream cheese, softened
4 12″ x 16″ sheets of *phylo* or strudel leaves
2 tablespoons melted butter
¼ cup bread crumbs

1. In the vegetable oil, sauté the sausage until it is evenly browned, about ten minutes. Remove the sausage with a slotted spoon and set aside.

2. In the same skillet sauté the onion, garlic, and mushrooms until soft, about ten minutes. Remove the mixture to the bowl with the sausage.

3. Add the parsley and cream cheese and mix well.

4. Lay one sheet of *phylo* on a counter top and brush it with some of the melted butter. Sprinkle some of the bread crumbs evenly over the sheet of *phylo*. Add another sheet on top of the first, brush with butter, and dust with crumbs. Continue in the same manner with the third and fourth sheets.

5. Spread the sausage mixture evenly over the top sheet of *phylo*, leaving a 1½-inch border all around. Tuck in the sides.

6. Carefully roll up the *phylo*, jelly roll fashion. Place the roll seam side down on a lightly greased jelly roll pan. Bake in a preheated 400° F oven for about fifteen minutes, or until the strudel is evenly browned. Cool slightly before slicing.

Serves 6 to 8 as an appetizer.

# Sausage Meals

One of the marvelous things about sausage is that it is so eminently adaptable. There is hardly a vegetable or fruit that doesn't go well with some kind of sausage. Part of sausage's versatility stems from the fact that it can be prepared in so many different ways. There isn't a single cuisine in the civilized world that doesn't include as part of its repertoire at least some kind of sausage.

There can be no such thing as the definitive sausage recipe book. For every idea about how to use sausage, there is an infinite number of variations around that theme. One needn't be a culinary genius to come up with one's own variations.

In this section, we are going to treat sausage as the main ingredient in a meal. It is as easy to construct an entire meal around sausage as it is to make sausage in the first place.

# Sausage and Eggs

## Country-Style Eggs with Sausage

*If there is anything more versatile than sausage, it would have to be the egg. Here is a simple recipe for one serving that uses both; it may be expanded for as many people as you have to serve.*

¼ pound country-style bulk
  sausage
2 eggs, well beaten
1 tablespoon milk
1 teaspoon fresh snipped
  chives
1 tablespoon grated Parmesan
  cheese
Salt to taste, if desired
Freshly ground black pepper

1. Sauté the sausage until it is browned, about ten minutes. Drain off almost all the grease.
2. In a mixing bowl, combine the eggs, milk, chives, cheese, salt, and pepper. Mix well.
3. Over medium heat, pour the scrambled egg mixture into the skillet with the sausage, stirring constantly until the eggs are set.

## Sausage and Mushroom Omelet

*Of all the things you can do with eggs, the omelet has to be one of the most perfect. The quintessential omelet is light, fluffy, and sweetly laced with butter. And yet many people shy away from making omelets because they think that they are difficult. Making a perfect omelet takes only a little patience and effort than perfectly scrambling an egg. Fillings for omelets are limited only by your tastes and imagination. The ingredients in this recipe make one serving.*

¼ pound bulk sausage
  (whatever kind you like)
2 tablespoons butter
1 tablespoon finely minced
  onion
¼ cup chopped fresh
  mushrooms
2 eggs
2 tablespoons milk
Salt to taste, if desired
Freshly ground black pepper

1. In a small skillet or omelet pan, sauté the sausage until it is browned. Remove the sausage with a slotted spoon and discard the drippings.
2. Melt the butter in the skillet and add the onion and mushrooms. Sauté until the onions are translucent and the mushrooms have given up some of their juice.
3. While the onions and mushrooms are cooking, beat the eggs until they are frothy. Stir in the milk, salt, and pepper.
4. When the onions and mushrooms are ready, pour the eggs into the pan over them. Cook the omelet over medium heat, tilting the pan and lifting the omelet's edges now and then to allow the uncooked mixture on the surface to flow underneath. When the omelet is almost set, sprinkle the sausage on one side of the omelet and fold it over. Serve immediately. Garnish with parsley if desired.

# Sausage Quiche

*The best excuse I can think of for using up a few eggs is to make a quiche. A quiche is a French pie. You have no doubt heard of and probably tasted a quiche Lorraine, which is a rich concoction of custard, cheese, and bacon. This dish is a variation on that theme. My sister is fond of dividing the mixed ingredients for a quiche and making small individual servings to use as an appetizer. This recipe may certainly be adapted to that end should you so desire, simply by using small tart shells instead of a pie plate. Dieters be warned: this dish is absolutely guaranteed to blow any diet—past, present or future!*

**For the pastry:**

1 cup sifted flour
¼ teaspoon salt
⅓ cup vegetable shortening
4 tablespoons (approximately) cold water

1. Sift the flour together with the salt.
2. Cut the shortening into marble-sized pieces and mix it into the flour with a pastry blender.
3. Sprinkle the water on a little at a time while mixing continuously with the pastry blender. Make the dough into a ball.
4. Roll the pastry out into a circle large enough to cover a nine-inch pie plate with the edges overlapping. Line the pie plate with the pastry and trim the edges.

**And now for the filling:**

½ pound bulk Italian-style sweet sausage
½ pound fresh mushrooms, sliced
1 small onion, chopped
½ small sweet green pepper, cored, seeded, and chopped
3 eggs, well beaten
2 cups half and half
4 ounces mozzarella or Gruyere cheese, shredded
¼ cup Romano cheese, grated
Dash of cayenne pepper
Salt to taste, if desired
Freshly ground black pepper

1. Sauté the sausage in a skillet until it loses its pink color. Remove it with a slotted spoon and set it aside.
2. In the sausage drippings, sauté the mushrooms, onions, and peppers until they are crisp-tender. Remove them with a slotted spoon and set them aside. Discard the drippings.
3. Beat the eggs, and while you continue to beat, add the half and half, cayenne, salt, and pepper.
4. Put the sausage into the pastry shell. Layer the onion, mushroom, and pepper mixture evenly over the sausage. Spread the grated cheeses over all. Finally, pour the egg and cream mixture over everything.
5. Bake in a preheated 400° F oven for about thirty minutes. Allow the *quiche* to cool for about ten minutes before slicing.

**Note:** to make individual *quiches*, simply divide the pastry and ingredients among as many tart shells as you plan to use.

Serves 4 as an entrée, 6 to 10 as an appetizer.

## Sausage Pipérade

*According to the* Larousse Gastronomique *a pipérade is a Basque dish of tomatoes and peppers to which eggs are added, one at a time, to obtain a fluffy puree. This recipe is a variation on that theme.*

1 pound bulk Italian-style
  sweet sausage
1 small onion, finely chopped
4 cloves garlic, finely chopped
2 tablespoons olive or vegetable
  oil
½ cup chopped red sweet
  pepper
½ cup chopped yellow sweet
  pepper
½ cup chopped green sweet
  pepper
2 tablespoons chopped fresh
  jalapeño pepper (or other hot
  green chili pepper)
½ teaspoon dried basil
½ teaspoon dried oregano
½ teaspoon dried thyme
½ teaspoon dried summer
  savory
½ teaspoon dried marjoram
½ teaspoon dried rosemary,
  crumbled
½ teaspoon dried sage
8 eggs
Salt to taste, if desired
Freshly ground black pepper

1. Sauté the sausage in a skillet over medium heat until it is lightly browned. Remove it with a slotted spoon. Discard the drippings.

2. In the skillet, heat the oil and sauté the onion and garlic until they are translucent.

3. Add the sweet and hot peppers to the skillet and sauté for five minutes.

4. Add the sausage and the remaining ingredients except the eggs, and cook, stirring, until the vegetables are soft, about ten minutes.

5. Divide the mixture among four individual ramekins. Make two indentations in the sausage mixture in each ramekin, and crack an egg into each indentation.

6. Bake the *pipérades* in a preheated 375° F oven for ten to twelve minutes or until the eggs are set.

Serves 4.

## Sausage, Chicken Livers, and Eggs

*Use the freshest chicken livers in this recipe and you will be rewarded with the most exquisite flavor.*

½ pound bulk country or other
  style sausage
1 tablespoon butter
½ pound fresh chicken livers,
  rinsed, patted dry, and
  coarsely chopped
1 tablespoon chopped chives
8 eggs, well beaten
Salt to taste, if desired
Freshly ground black pepper

1. Sauté the sausage until it is browned. Remove it with a slotted spoon and set it aside. Discard the drippings.

2. Add the butter to the skillet and sauté the chopped chicken livers for four to five minutes.

3. Return the sausage to the skillet. Add the chives and the eggs, salt, and pepper. Stir constantly over medium heat until the eggs are fluffy and well scrambled.

Serves 4.

# Sausage Crêpes

*Crêpes* are fun food, and at the same time, they are very elegant. My son, Chuck, used to call them "creeps," but since he discovered April in Paris, he also discovered the true pronounciation.

*Crêpes* are very thin pancakes. They can be made in a variety of ways. The easiest way to make them is probably with an electric *crêpe* maker, but a non-stick skillet will do just as well.

## Basic Italian Cheese Crêpe Batter

1 cup all-purpose flour
1½ cups milk
2 eggs
2 tablespoons Parmesan cheese
2 tablespoons Romano cheese
1 tablespoon olive or vegetable oil

1. Mix all the ingredients together in a bowl and beat until the batter is smooth.

2. If you are using an electric *crêpe* maker, follow the manufacturer's directions. Otherwise, lightly grease a skillet and preheat it for a couple of minutes.

3. Add about two tablespoons of batter to the pan and spread it to the edges. Brown one side of the *crêpe*. The top side will be firm (not wet) to the touch when the *crêpe* is done. Repeat until all the batter is used. Stack the cooked *crêpes* between paper toweling or waxed paper.

## Dagwood Crêpe Sandwich

*This is a knife-and-fork sandwich which can be a showcase for several of your homemade sausages. Dagwood Bumstead would be in heaven if he found the ingredients for this dish lying in the back of the refrigerator at three in the morning.*

1 dozen basic Italian cheese *crêpes*
1 dozen thin slices *each* of three or four different cured sausages
1 medium onion thinly sliced
½ cup sliced stuffed green olives
¼ cup chopped dill pickle
¼ cup herbed salad dressing (See step 3)
6 slices Swiss cheese

1. Prepare the *crêpes*.

2. Arrange half the *crêpes* on a baking sheet. Layer half the sausages, onion, olive, and pickle on these *crêpes*. Repeat layers with remaining *crêpes* and ingredients.

3. Mixed the herbed salad dressing as follows: to three tablespoons of red wine vinegar, add ½ teaspoon sugar, ½ teaspoon salt, ¼ teaspoon each of oregano, basil, and thyme, a dash of cayenne, and freshly ground black pepper to taste. Add one tablespoon olive oil and shake vigorously. Sprinkle an equal amount of dressing on each *crêpe* sandwich.

4. Top each sandwich with a slice of Swiss cheese and bake in a preheated 400° F oven for about ten minutes or until the cheese is melted.

Serves 6.

## Baked Italian Sausage Crêpes

*This dish is very similar to an Italian dish called Baked Stuffed Manicotti which consists of large tubular pieces of pasta stuffed with various fillings.*

1 dozen Italian Cheese *crêpes*
1½ pounds Italian-style hot or sweet sausage removed from the casing
1 small onion, chopped
12 ounces fresh mushrooms, chopped
8 ounces mozzarella cheese, shredded
2 eggs well beaten
1 egg well beaten
4 cups tomato sauce
¼ cup grated Parmesan cheese
Salt to taste, if desired
Freshly ground black pepper
Chopped fresh parsley to garnish

1. Prepare the *crêpes* according to the basic recipe and set aside.
2. Sauté the sausage until it is lightly browned. Remove it with a slotted spoon.
3. Sauté the onions and mushrooms in the sausage drippings until the onion is translucent. Remove with a slotted spoon to the bowl with the sausage.
4. Add the mozzarella and two beaten eggs to the sausage mixture and mix through well.
5. Brush each *crêpe* with the remaining beaten egg. Divide the sausage mixture among the *crêpes*. Place the filling on half of the *crêpes* only and leave a one-inch border.
6. Fold the bare half of each *crêpe* over the filling and press the edges down firmly.
7. Spread half of the tomato sauce in the bottom of a baking pan. Place the *crêpes* in a single layer on top of the sauce. Pour the rest of the sauce over the *crêpes* and sprinkle on the Parmesan cheese.
8. Bake in a preheated 400° F oven, covered, for about thirty minutes or until the sauce is bubbly and the *crêpes* are heated through.
9. Garnish with the parsley and serve hot.
Serves 4.

## Breakfast Sausage Sandwich Crêpes

*This is a new way to have your pancakes and sausage for breakfast. Use the basic* crêpe *batter, but leave out the grated cheeses.*

1 dozen *crêpes*
1 pound country-style bulk sausage
Maple syrup

1. Prepare the *crêpes* and keep them warm.
2. Sauté the sausage in a skillet until it is well browned. Remove it with a slotted spoon and keep it warm.
3. Layer the *crêpes* and sausage on individual plates. Pass the syrup at the table.
Serves 4.

## Salami Crêpes

*This is a good dish to serve at a luncheon.*

**1 dozen Italian cheese** *crêpes*
**Dijon-style mustard**
**¼ pound thinly sliced home-made hard salami**
**¼ pound Swiss cheese, shredded**

1. Prepare the *crêpes.*
2. Spread a thin layer of mustard on each *crêpe.*
3. Layer equal amounts of salami and cheese on each *crêpe.* Roll up the *crêpes* jelly roll fashion.
4. Arrange the *crêpes* on a cookie sheet and bake in a preheated 425° F oven for ten minutes or until the cheese is melted.

Serves 4.

## Sausage, Onion, and Pepper Crêpes

*Here is a classic combination in a new wrapping.*

**1 dozen Italian cheese** *crêpes*
**¾ pound sweet Italian-style sausage removed from the casing**
**1 small onion, chopped**
**1 small sweet green pepper, cored, seeded, and chopped**

1. Prepare the *crêpes.*
2. Sauté the sausage in a skillet until it is browned. Remove it with a slotted spoon and divide it equally among the *crêpes.*
3. In the sausage drippings sauté the onion and pepper until they are crisp-tender, about five minutes. Remove with a slotted spoon and divide among the *crêpes.*
4. Roll up the *crêpes* and place on a greased cookie sheet. Bake in a preheated 425° F oven for about ten minutes or until warmed through.

Serves 4.

# Sausage and Apples

*Pork and apples are a natural go-together. The tartness of the apples contrasts with the mildness of the meat, bringing out the best in both. Any fresh pork sausages in this book can be used to advantage with apples to create a hearty and satisfying meal.*

## Sausage and Apple Pancakes

*Sausages and pancakes go together like bread and butter. Pancake rollups, stuffed with sausage and apples, with some real down-home maple syrup dribbled on top make for a super breakfast dish or a quick supper. Make your own pancakes from scratch, using the recipe here or use your own favorite mix.*

1 pound bulk country-style
   pork sausage
2 large apples, peeled, cored,
   and chopped coarsely
½ cup apple jelly
2 eggs, well beaten
1½ cups milk
2 tablespoons melted butter or
   vegetable oil
2 cups sifted all-purpose flour
3 teaspoons baking powder
Salt to taste, if desired

1. Brown the sausage in a large skillet. Drain off the fat.
2. Add the apples and cook until tender.
3. Stir in the apple jelly. Remove from heat and keep warm.
4. Mix together the eggs, milk, and butter or oil. Sift in the flour, baking powder, and salt. Beat until the mixture is smooth and free of lumps.
5. Make the pancakes in a lightly oiled griddle. As each one is done, spoon some of the sausage mixture on it, roll it up, dribble on some maple syrup, and serve immediately.

Serves 4.

## Sausage-Stuffed Apples

*Nothing chases away the chill of a cool, crisp autumn evening like big juicy apples begging to be stuffed and baked.*

1 pound fresh bulk pork
   sausage
1 small onion, finely chopped
1 cup chopped celery
3–5 cups soft bread crumbs
   (the amount depends on how
   big the apples are)
½ cup hot water
½ cup dry white wine

Optional seasonings (depending on what kind of sausage
you are using):
½ teaspoon thyme
½ teaspoon sage
½ teaspoon marjoram
½ teaspoon cinnamon
¼ teaspoon ground allspice
6 very large baking apples
   (Golden Delicious, Cortland,
   Rome, Winesap, Northern
   Spy, McIntosh)

1. Brown the sausage lightly in a skillet. Remove it with a slotted spoon and set it aside.
2. In the drippings, sauté the onion and celery until they are crisp-tender. Drain off the fat.
3. Return the sausage to the skillet and add all the remaining ingredients except the apples. Mix well and remove from the heat.
4. Core the apples and peel each one about a third of the way down. Stuff the centers of the apples with equal amounts of the sausage mixture.
5. Place the stuffed apples in a greased baking pan and bake in a preheated 375° F oven for about forty-five minutes or until the apples are tender.

Serves 6.

## Sausage and Apple Roll

*This is a meat roll which bakes up like a meat loaf.*

**2 pounds fresh bulk pork
   sausage**
**3 medium apples, peeled,
   cored, and chopped**
**1 small onion, coarsely
   chopped**
**1½ cups fresh bread crumbs**
**¼ teaspoon nutmeg (optional)**
**¼ teaspoon ground allspice
   (optional)**
**Dash of cayenne pepper
   (optional)**
**Salt to taste, if desired**
**Freshly ground black pepper**

1. On a large piece of waxed paper or plastic wrap, spread out the sausage in the form of a rectangle about a half an inch thick.

2. In a mixing bowl, combine the remaining ingredients.

3. Spread the apple mixture over the sausage, leaving an inch-wide border all the way around.

4. Roll up the sausage jelly roll fashion. Begin by picking up one end of the paper or plastic wrap and folding it over until the roll gets started. The meat should fall away from the paper or wrap easily. When the roll is complete, pinch the ends together to seal.

5. Place the roll on a greased pan and bake in a preheated 375° F oven for one hour.

Serves 8.

## (Sausage and?) Apple Pie

*Why not? Instead of a traditional "crust" for this pie, we are going to use a bed of mashed potatoes. Voila! A one-dish meal that is as satisfying as it is delicious.*

**1 pound fresh bulk
   pork sausage**
**1 large onion, finely chopped**
**½ cup chopped celery**
**2 large apples, peeled, cored,
   and thinly sliced**
**8 ounces coarsely chopped
   fresh mushrooms**
**Optional seasonings (pick and
choose):**
   **1 teaspoon dillweed**
   **½ teaspoon marjoram**
   **½ teaspoon ground allspice**
   **1 teaspoon mint**
   **2 tablespoons parsley**
**¼ cup brandy**
**4 tablespoons butter or
   margarine**
**4 tablespoons flour**
**2 cups milk**
**3 cups mashed potatoes**
**1 egg, well beaten**
**Salt to taste, if desired**
**Freshly ground black pepper**

1. Crumble the sausage in a large skillet and lightly brown it over medium heat.

2. Add the onion, celery, apples, and mushrooms and continue cooking until all are crisp-tender.

3. Add any of the optional seasonings and brandy and cook until most of the liquid has evaporated, about ten minutes. Remove from heat, but keep warm.

4. Drain off the sausage drippings. In a small saucepan, heat the four tablespoons of butter or margarine and combine with the flour. Simmer and stir until you have a fine *roux*. Remove from heat and slowly add the milk, stirring constantly. Cook over moderate heat, stirring, until the sauce thickens. Pour the sauce into the sausage mixture and stir well.

5. Prepare the mashed potatoes and stir in the egg. Add salt and pepper to taste.

6. Fill a greased two-quart casserole with about half of the mashed potatoes. Spoon in the sausage mixture and top with the remaining potatoes.

7. Bake, uncovered, in a preheated 425° F oven for about twenty-five minutes or until the top is well browned. Serve hot.

Serves 4 to 6.

# Sausage with Pasta, Noodles, and Dumplings

Whole cuisines have been built around the noodle. The one that comes to mind first is probably Italian. Certainly the Italians have carried the noodle experience to its outer limits. Whether the dough is for noodles or dumplings, sausage provides a perfect counterpoint to the taste and texture. Here are some examples.

## Piroghi

*Piroghi (or pirohi, or piroshki or any one of at least a half dozen other spellings) are a Russian dish, filled dumplings made from a raised dough. Technically, they aren't a pasta or noodle dish, but the dough is similar.*

**For the dough:**

½ cup lukewarm water
1 (¼ ounce) package dry yeast
2½ cups sifted all purpose
   flour
1 egg, well beaten
2 tablespoons vegetable oil

**For the filling:**

1 pound fresh bulk sausage,
   any variety
1 small onion, chopped
1 egg, well beaten
Melted butter or margarine
Chopped fresh parsley

1. Mix the yeast with one half cup of lukewarm water and let it rest for fifteen minutes or until it becomes frothy.

2. Add the yeast to the flour with the remaining dough ingredients and mix to make a soft dough.

3. Place the dough in a greased bowl, cover and let the dough double in size.

4. While the dough is rising, sauté the sausage until it is lightly browned. Remove it with a slotted spoon and set it aside.

5. In the drippings, sauté the onion until it is tender. Remove with a slotted spoon.

6. Mix the sausage, onion, and beaten egg until thoroughly blended.

7. Punch down the dough and roll it out on a floured surface until it is about an eighth of an inch thick. Cut it into circles about three inches in diameter.

8. Place about a tablespoon of the sausage mixture on each circle of dough and fold over to form half moons. Pinch the edges tightly to seal.

9. Place the *piroghi*, a few at a time, in a large pot of boiling water and boil three to four minutes. When all the piroghi are done, put them in a large bowl, toss them with butter, parsley, salt, and pepper and serve warm.

Serves 4 to 6.

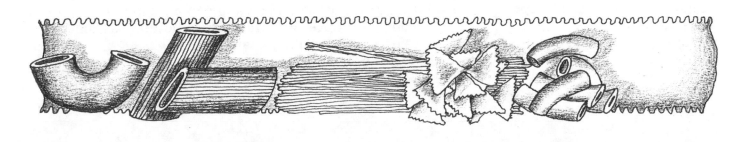

## Lasagna Rollups with Sausage

*My sister Renée invented lasagna rollups as an elegant but quick company dish to serve a crowd. She uses a ricotta filling (delicious!) whereas this recipe uses (how did you guess?) your homemade Italian sausage.*

1½ pounds hot or sweet Italian-style sausage
8 ounces mozzarella cheese, shredded
1 egg, well beaten
6 cups tomato sauce
½ cup freshly grated Parmesan cheese
2 tablespoons chopped parsley
Salt to taste, if desired
Freshly ground black pepper

1. Sauté the sausage meat until it loses its pink color. Drain with a slotted spoon.
2. Mix together the sausage, mozzarella, and egg.
3. Cook the lasagna noddles according to package directions.
4. Spread one cup of the tomato sauce evenly on the bottom of a lasagna or baking pan.
5. Lay a lasagna noodle on a flat surface and spread some of the sausage mixture thinly on the length of the noodle. Roll up the noodle jelly roll fashion.
6. Proceed with the rest of the noodles and filling in the same manner. Lay the rollups, seam side down, in the baking pan and pour the rest of the sauce over them.
7. Sprinkle the Parmesan cheese over all and bake in a preheated 425° F oven, covered, for thirty minutes or until the sauce is bubbly. Garnish with parsley and serve.
Serves 10 to 12.

## Scampi Sausage with Fettuccine

*Linguine or fettuccine are the traditional pasta accompaniments to an Italian fish sauce because their shape allows the delicate sauce to better coat the noodle. Use either in this recipe, but the fettuccine, because it is slightly wider, does provide a slightly better foil to the sausage.*

2 cloves garlic, finely minced
2 tablespoons olive oil
¼ cup shallots, finely chopped
¼ cup finely minced fresh parsley
2 pounds scampi sausage
1 cup dry white wine
3 cups tomato sauce
Salt to taste, if desired
Freshly ground black pepper
1 pound fettuccine

1. Sauté the garlic in the oil until it is lightly browned. Discard it.
2. Sauté the shallots in the olive oil until they are softened, about five minutes. Add the parsley and stir.
3. Add the scampi sausage and sauté, turning the sausages, until they are lightly browned all over.
4. Add the wine, tomato sauce, salt, and pepper. Simmer ten minutes.
5. Meanwhile, cook the fettucine in rapidly boiling water. Drain, toss with butter, and arrange on a platter.
6. Pour the sauce over the fettuccine and arrange the sausages on top. Serve immediately.
Serves 6 to 8.

# Lasagna with Sausage

*If there ever were a party dish for a crowd, lasagna is it.*

2 tablespoons olive oil
1 pound bulk Italian-style sweet sausage
8 cups tomato sauce (your own favorite or use the recipe on p. 125)
3 eggs well beaten
1 large (46 ounce) container ricotta cheese (may be part skim)
¼ cup chopped fresh parsley
Salt to taste, if desired
Freshly ground black pepper
1 pound lasagna noodles
1 12-ounce package mozzarella cheese
1 cup freshly grated Parmesan cheese
1 cup freshly grated Romano cheese

1. In a large, deep skillet or a Dutch oven, heat the olive oil and brown the sausage. Pour off all but two tablespoons of the drippings.

2. Add the tomato sauce and bring to a simmer.

3. Bring a large pot of water to a boil.

4. In a mixing bowl, combine the eggs, ricotta, parsley, salt, and pepper.

5. Cook the lasagna noodles in the boiling water according to package directions. Drain.

6. In a lasagna pan, spread a thin layer of sauce. Add a layer of noodles. Spread some of the ricotta mixture evenly over the noodles. Sprinkle about a quarter of the mozzarella, Parmesan, and Romano cheeses over the ricotta. Add a layer of sauce and continue layering until all the ingredients are used. Reserve the leftover sauce to pass at the table. End with a layer of sauce.

7. Bake, covered, in a preheated 425° F oven for forty minutes or until the lasagna is bubbly.

Serving suggestion: for hearty appetites, broil some Italian-style sausage links to serve with the lasagna. A tossed green salad and a *classico reserve Chianti* would make this a meal to remember.

Serves 10 to 12.

# Sausage and Rigatoni

*This is a classic combination.*

1 tablespoon olive oil
1 pound sweet Italian-style sausage links
1 small onion, chopped
1 small sweet green pepper, seeded, cored, and chopped
4 cups tomato sauce
1 tablespoon chopped parsley
1 pound cooked rigatoni
1 12-ounce package mozzarella cheese, shredded
½ cup Romano cheese, grated

1. Cook the sausages in the olive oil in a large skillet until they are lightly browned. Set the sausages aside to cool slightly and drain off all but two tablespoons of the drippings.

2. Sauté the onion and pepper until they are crisp-tender.

3. Add the tomato sauce and parsley and simmer over medium heat until heated through.

4. Slice the sausages into one-inch pieces and add them to the sauce. Simmer for ten minutes.

5. Cook the rigatoni according to package directions and drain.

6. In a greased baking dish arrange layers of sauce, rigatoni, and mozzarella cheese. Sprinkle the Romano cheese on top.

7. Bake, uncovered, in a preheated 425° F oven until the sauce is bubbly and the top layer of cheese is slightly browned, about twenty minutes.

Serves 4 to 6.

# Ravioli with Sausage

*Here the sausage is in the sauce and serves as a flavorful counterpoint to the mildly herbed filling of the ravioli.*

*If you have never made your own ravioli, now is the time to give it a try because they are easy to make, inexpensive, and delicious. You can make your own ravioli the old fashioned way, using a rolling pin, teaspoon, and knife, or you can invest about $10 in a ravioli maker. This device is well worth the money because it simplifies the job and practically guarantees success.*

*If you are going to make your own ravioli, or any pasta, be sure to use real semolina flour. Many published recipes for homemade pasta call for all-purpose flour, but for the best taste and texture, the real thing can't be beat. Semolina, the purified middlings of hard wheat, such as durum, is more yellow and coarser than all-purpose flour.*

**For the dough:**

**2½ cups semolina flour**
**1 teaspoon salt (not so much for flavor as texture)**
**2 eggs, well beaten**
**Water**

1. Mix the semolina and salt.
2. Make a well in the center of the semolina which should be mounded on a pastry board.
3. Pour the beaten eggs into the well and mix the eggs into the flour a little at a time.
4. Add a little water, gradually, to make the dough work up into a ball. Knead it, using additional flour if necessary, until you have a stiff but pliable ball of dough. Place the dough in a bowl and cover it with a cloth until you are ready to use it.

At this point you must decide whether you want a meat or cheese filling.

**For the cheese filling:**

**1 pound ricotta cheese**
**½ pound shredded mozzarella cheese**
**½ cup grated Romano or Parmesan cheese**
**½ cup finely chopped Italian parsley**
**2 eggs, well beaten**
**Salt to taste, if desired**
**Freshly ground black pepper**

In a large mixing bowl combine all the ingredients and blend well.

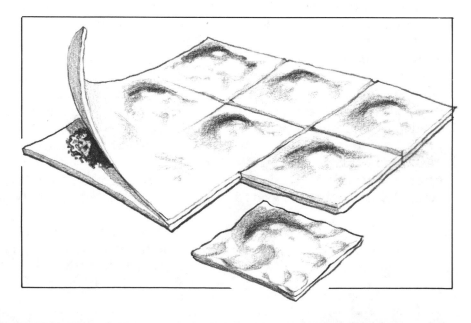

**For the meat filling:**

½ pound finely ground beef
½ pound finely ground pork
½ pound finely ground veal
¼ cup grated Romano cheese
1 clove garlic, finely minced
2 tablespoons onion, finely
   minced
½ teaspoon basil
¼ teaspoon nutmeg
2 eggs, well beaten
¼ cup finely chopped parsley
Salt to taste, if desired
Freshly ground black pepper

**For the sauce:**

1 pound sweet Italian-style
   sausage removed from the
   casing and crumbled
4 cups tomato sauce
½ cup grated Romano cheese
½ cup grated Parmesan cheese
2 tablespoons chopped parsley
Salt to taste, if desired
Freshly ground black pepper

In a large mixing bowl combine all the ingredients.

To make the ravioli, if you are using a ravioli maker, roll a piece of dough about the size of a lemon out on a floured board to about the thickness of a knife blade (between an eighth and sixteenth of an inch). Place this piece of dough on the serrated plate of the ravioli maker. Repeat the process with another piece of dough. Spoon about a teaspoon of filling into each indentation of the first piece of dough and place the second piece on top of the first piece. Roll across the top sheet of dough with a rolling pin to seal the edges and cut the ravioli apart.

If you do not have a ravioli maker, proceed as follows:

Roll out the first piece of dough as in the above instructions. Lay it flat on a floured board. Place about a teaspoon of filling in a grid pattern about 1½ inches square. Place the second sheet of dough on top of the first sheet and press down around the sides of each mound of filling to form squares. With a serrated edge pastry cutter cut between the squares.

With either method, repeat the process until all the dough and filling are used. This recipe yields about six dozen ravioli.

Set the ravioli aside on a floured surface while you assemble the sauce. (The ravioli may be frozen at this point if you want to use them at a later date.)

1. Crumble the sausage meat in a deep skillet and sauté it over medium heat until it is lightly browned.

2. Add the tomato sauce and gently simmer until it is bubbly, about twenty minutes.

3. Boil the ravioli gently in salted water for four or five minutes. Drain.

4. Layer the sauce, ravioli, and grated cheese in individual ramekins or in a large baking dish. Bake, uncovered, in a preheated 400° F oven for about fifteen minutes or until the sauce is bubbly. Garnish with chopped parsley and serve.

Serves 4 to 6.

## Macaroni and Hot Dogs

*This dish isn't exactly company fare but kids love it. It is perfect for a blustery winter's evening when you don't have a lot of time to cook.*

2 tablespoons vegetable oil
1 pound homemade hot dogs
¼ cup chopped onion
2 cloves minced garlic
4 cups tomato sauce
1 teaspoon oregano
1 pound elbow or ditalini
  macaroni
Salt to taste, if desired
Freshly ground black pepper

1. Bring four quarts of water to a boil and cook the macaroni according to package directions. Drain.
2. While the macaroni is cooking, heat the oil in a large skillet and add the hot dogs (cut into one-inch pieces), the onion, and garlic. Sauté until the hot dogs are lightly browned.
3. Add the tomato sauce and mix well.
4. Add the oregano, salt, and pepper.
5. Add the cooked macaroni to the sauce and cook over medium heat until heated through, about two minutes.
Serves 4 to 6.

## Sausage-Stuffed Egg Rolls

*Commercially prepared egg roll skins will work very well in this recipe.*

For the filling:
½ pound bulk fresh country-
  style sausage (or any other
  mildly flavored sausage)
1 cup finely chopped celery
1 cup finely shredded cabbage
1 cup finely chopped green
  onions
½ cup finely shredded carrots
½ cup finely chopped mushrooms
¼ cup finely chopped sweet
  green pepper
2 teaspoons Worcestershire
  sauce
1 egg
Salt to taste, if desired
Freshly ground white pepper
1 egg white

1. Sauté the sausage in a skillet over medium heat until it is lightly browned. Drain off most of the fat.
2. Add all the remaining ingredients except the egg white, mix well, and sauté two minutes, stirring. Remove the mixture from the heat and allow it to cool.
3. To assemble the egg rolls, place about a quarter cup of the filling in the center of an egg roll skin and fold two sides over to the center. Brush the two sides and the two open sides with the egg white and roll up the skin. Carefully place the egg rolls on a baking pan and refrigerate for two hours.
4. Deep fat fry the egg rolls until they are crisp and golden.
Serve with Chinese (hot) mustard or your favorite dipping sauce.
You can make smaller versions of these egg rolls to serve as *hors d'oeuvres* by using smaller *won ton* skins.

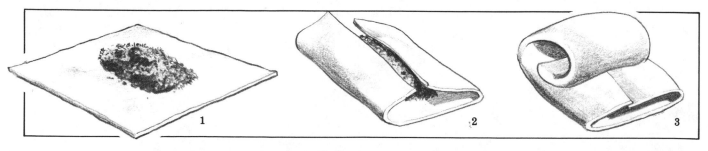

# Sausage with Poultry

We have come a long way from the days of a chicken in every pot on Sunday. There was a time when poultry graced the table only when the old hen stopped laying because it was too precious to kill and cook while it could still produce.

Generally, when meat prices spiral upward, poultry remains one of the biggest bargains in the meat case. Not only is it economical, but it can be prepared in a most elegant manner. Chicken and sausage are naturals to go together because both are so entirely versatile. Try some of the following combinations and see if you don't agree.

## Chicken and Sausage Cacciatore

*Cacciatore means something fixed "in the style of the hunter." This dish need not be complicated. Elegant, yes. But true to its name it should be easily assembled and passed quickly from stove to table.*

¼ cup vegetable or olive oil
1 three-pound broiler-fryer cut into serving pieces
1 pound hot or sweet Italian-style sausage links
1 medium onion, sliced thinly
2 cloves garlic, minced
1 medium green, yellow or red sweet pepper, cut into quarter-inch strips
4 cups Italian plum tomatoes, peeled, cored, seeded, and chopped
2 teaspoons oregano
1 teaspoon basil
1 bay leaf
1 whole hot red pepper pod or one teaspoon crushed red pepper
Salt to taste, if desired
Freshly ground black pepper
1 pound spaghetti or spahettini
Chopped parsley
Parmesan Cheese

1. In a large skillet, brown the chicken in the oil, about twenty minutes. Remove the chicken and keep it warm.

2. Brown the sausages in the same skillet, about twenty minutes. Remove and keep warm.

3. Discard all but two tablespoons of the accumulated drippings. Add the onion, garlic, and pepper, and sauté until the onions and peppers are crisp-tender.

4. Add the chopped tomatoes, oregano, basil, bay leaf, pepper pod, salt, and pepper. Bring the sauce to a simmer and return the chicken to the sauce. Simmer for thirty minutes.

5. Bring a large pot of water to a boil to cook the pasta.

6. When the water is ready, remove the meat from the sauce and keep it warm.

7. Cook the pasta according to package directions, drain and toss with a small amount of butter. Place the pasta on a large platter. Arrange the meat on top of the pasta and pour the sauce over all. Sprinkle the Parmesan cheese on top and garnish with the chopped parsley.

Serves 6 to 8.

# Chicken Stuffed with Sausage and Czech Dressing

*This is an excellent company dish which at first may seem difficult to prepare, but it really isn't. You are either going to have to prevail upon your friendly butcher to prepare the chicken for this dish or follow the instructions here for boning out the bird.*

*If you have never had a whole boneless chicken, you are in for a real treat. You might think at first that a chicken without bones can't look much like a real chicken, but this isn't the case at all. It not only looks like a whole roasted chicken, but it carves like a roast, which means no intricate carving calesthenics at the table. All the intricacies are taken care of before the bird sees the inside of an oven.*

1 5–7 pound roasting chicken, boned
Salt to taste, if desired
Chicken giblets (heart, gizzard, and liver from the roaster)
2 tablespoons olive or vegetable oil
¼ cup chopped celery
¼ cup chopped onion
1 clove garlic, minced
1 four- to five-inch link Italian, Polish, Spanish or other spicy sausage
2 cups, approximately, fresh bread crumbs
2 tablespoons grated carrot
½ cup dry white wine
¼ teaspoon ground allspice
¼ teaspoon dry sage
¼ teaspoon dry thyme
1 tablespoon chopped parsley
1 teaspoon Worcestershire sauce
Dash of Tabasco
2 teaspoons crushed rosemary
Salt to taste, if desired
Freshly ground black pepper

Here is how to bone the roaster:

1. Place the chicken on a cutting board so that the back is facing up. Cut down the center line of the backbone from the neck to the tail. Use a sharp knife. As you work at this, remember that time is not of the essence. The chicken isn't going to get up and go anywhere so take your time and you'll do a creditable job the first time.

2. With a pair of heavy-duty kitchen scissors, cut the entire backbone. Make the cut about one inch to either side of the center line. Remove the backbone, cut it in half, and reserve it along with the giblets.

3. You are now gazing into a spineless bird. You'll notice that the breastbone, that's the bone opposite from the one you just removed, runs the length of the bird until it ends as a piece of white cartilage. Grasp both ends of the chicken and bend until the breastbone pops out and away from the cartilage.

4. Push the breast meat away from the bone until the rudder-shaped end of the bone (called the keel) is completely free of the meat.

5. With a sharp knife, gently "shave" the meat away from the rib bones in one piece. Work first down one side and then the other.

6. With the ribs free, split the cartilage at the first joint of the rib cage. *At all times be careful not to puncture the skin of the bird!*

7. Work the knife point into the joints where the wings are attached. Sever these joints, leaving the wings attached to the carcass by meat and skin. The wings themselves are not boned out.

8. Feel for the wish bone, make a wish, cut around it and remove it.

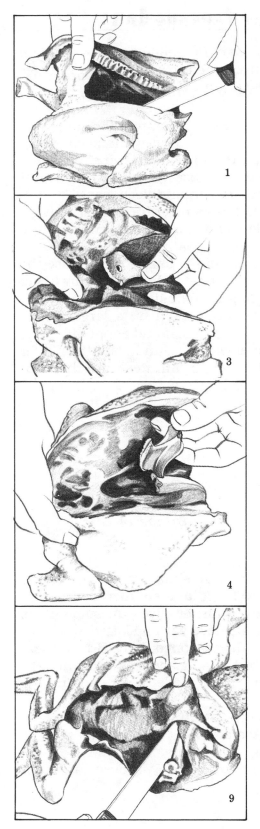

9. Feel for the thigh bones (no jokes here). Cut down the center of each thigh bone until you reach the leg joint. Shave the meat away from the thigh bones, sever the joint, lift out the bones but leave the drumsticks attached just the way you did the wings. The bird is now boned. Place it on a platter and refrigerate.

To prepare the dish:

1. Place all the bones in a stockpot along with the back and giblets. Cover them with cold water, add salt if desired, bring to a boil, reduce heat to a simmer and cook for forty-five minutes.

2. Heat the oil in a large skillet and add the celery, onion, garlic, and sausage link. Sauté until the vegetables are translucent and the sausage is lightly browned. Remove the sausage and set it aside.

3. Add the bread crumbs, carrot, wine, the remaining herbs except for the rosemary, the Worcestershire, and Tabasco. Mix well.

4. Chop the giblets into small pieces and, along with any meat you can scrape from the bones in the stock pot, add them to the skillet.

5. Place the chicken on the cutting board. Spread half of the stuffing mixture on the meat side of the spread-eagle bird. Don't get it too close to the edges. Place the sausage in the center. It should be almost as long as the inside of the carcass. Spread the rest of the stuffing on top of the sausage.

6. With poultry skewers and kitchen twine lace up the bird, being careful to tuck in the flaps of skin at both ends securely. Alternatively, you can "stitch" the bird up with twine and a large gauge sewing needle.

7. With a piece of twine about two feet long make a loop under each of the wings, Turn the bird over, crisscross the string and loop it over the drumsticks. Tie a secure knot. The chicken should now look more like the real thing. As it cooks, the chicken will shrink, the stuffing will expand and the bird will look perfectly true to form.

8. Place the bird in a roasting pan, breast side up, and insert a meat thermometer into the stuffing between the thigh and the breast. Sprinkle on the rosemary and salt and pepper to taste.

9. Roast, uncovered, in a preheated 375° F oven until the thermometer reads 170° F about 2½–3 hours. Baste it frequently with the pan juices.

10. After it is removed from the oven, let the chicken rest fifteen minutes before carving. Remove the wings and then slice, front to back just as you would a roast. Each slice is framed in chicken with a perfectly round piece of sausage in the center.

Serves 8 to 10.

## Chicken and Sausage Provençale

Provençale *means "in the style of Provence," a geographical and political region of France. In cooking terms, provençale usually means garlic, parsley, and white wine.*

2 tablespoons olive or vegetable
  oil
1 pound fresh garlic or sweet
  Italian-style sausage links
1 three-pound broiler-fryer
  chicken cut into serving
  pieces
½ cup flour
3 cloves garlic, finely minced
4 shallots, finely minced
1 cup dry white wine
½ cup chopped parsley
½ cup fine dry bread crumbs
Salt to taste, if desired
Freshly ground black pepper

1. Heat the oil in a large skillet and brown the sausages, about twenty minutes. Remove the sausages and keep warm.

2. Dredge the chicken parts in the flour and sauté them over medium high heat until they are golden brown, about twenty minutes. Remove the chicken and keep warm.

3. Drain off all but two tablespoons of the pan drippings. Add the garlic and the shallots and sauté them until they are slightly golden.

4. Add the wine and parsley to the skillet and reduce the liquid by half over medium high heat. Scrape the pan to get all the little brown bits clinging to the bottom.

5. Arrange the sausage and chicken on a large platter and pour the pan juices over all. Add salt and pepper to taste. Sprinkle the bread crumbs evenly over all and place the platter in a preheated broiler for about eight minutes until the meat is crisp and the juices are bubbling.

Serves 6 to 8.

## Sausage and Chicken Casserole

*Here is another perfect culinary marriage of chicken and sausage.*

1½ pounds any link spicy
  sausage
1 3-pound broiler-fryer cut into
  serving pieces
1 cup flour seasoned with salt
  and pepper
12 small potatoes, peeled
2 cups small onions, peeled
5 carrots cut into one-inch
  pieces (about two cups)
1 sweet red or green pepper
  cut into strips
2 whole tomatoes, peeled,
  cored, seeded, and chopped
2 cloves garlic, minced
1 teaspoon oregano
½ cup dry white wine

1. Put enough water in a large skillet to just cover the bottom. Add the sausage and bring to a simmer. Cook until the water evaporates and the sausage gives up some of its grease and begins to brown. Remove with a slotted spoon.

2. Dredge the chicken in the seasoned flour. Brown them in the sausage drippings. (If the sausage was exceptionally lean, add a little vegetable oil to the skillet before adding the chicken.)

3. Brown the potatoes with the chicken.

4. Put the meat in a casserole along with potatoes.

5. Add all the remaining ingredients.

6. Bake, covered, in a preheated 375° F oven for about sixty minutes.

Serves 4 to 6.

# Roast Duckling with Sausage

*Luganega sausage would be a good choice to use in this recipe because the lemony-orange flavors blend well with the duck.*

1 4—5 pound duckling with giblets
2½ cups dry red wine
½ cup duck broth (from cooking the giblets)
1 small onion, chopped
2 cloves garlic, minced
12 ounces fresh mushrooms, chopped
Salt to taste, if desired
Freshly ground black pepper
1 pound luganega sausage

1. Wash and pat the duckling dry. Cut it into quarters. Cut off as much fat from the tail section as possible. Prick the skin in several places to allow fat to escape while cooking.

2. Place the pieces of duckling on a rack in a shallow roasting pan and bake in a preheated 425° F oven, uncovered, for thirty minutes.

3. In a small saucepan, cook the giblets in ¾ cup water for thirty minutes. At the end of the cooking time, there should be about a half a cup of liquid remaining.

4. Remove the duckling from the oven, drain off the accumulated drippings, and place the pieces of duck on the bottom of the roasting pan.

5. Combine the wine, duck broth, garlic onion, mushrooms, salt, and pepper and pour this over the duckling. Add the sausage to the roasting pan.

6. Reduce oven heat to 375° F and roast, uncovered, for forty-five minutes.

7. Serve the pieces of duck and sausage on a platter with the wine sauce poured over them.

Serves 4 to 6.

# Duck Sausage Bourguignonne

*Classic* boeuf bourguignonne *derives its delicious flavor from slow simmering and lots of red wine. Although this recipe needs less simmering because the meat doesn't need tenderizing, the flavor is just as distinct.*

2 pounds duck sausage
3 tablespoons olive oil
6 cups thinly sliced onions
12 ounces fresh mushrooms, sliced
2 cloves garlic, finely minced
1 bay leaf
1 teaspoon thyme
1 teaspoon marjoram
2 cups dry red wine
2 cups chicken stock
1 tablespoon arrowroot
¼ cup brandy
Salt to taste, if desired
Freshly ground black pepper

1. In a large skillet, pour enough water to just cover the bottom and sauté the sausage until the water evaporates and the sausages are nicely browned. Remove the sausage with a slotted spoon and drain on paper toweling.

2. Heat the olive oil in a Dutch oven and sauté the onions and mushrooms until they are slightly wilted, about ten minutes.

3. Add the garlic, bay leaf, thyme, marjoram, wine and stock. Bring to a boil, reduce the heat, add the sausages and simmer for thirty minutes.

4. Mix the arrowroot with the brandy, bring the bourguignonne to a boil, and add the brandy, stirring, until the mixture thickens. Serve hot.

Serves 6.

## Stuffed Breast of Chicken

*Someone, some day, will undoubtedly try to catalogue everything that can be done with a breast of chicken. The French call a boneless breast of chicken a suprême which is appropriate because some of the world's most supremely elegant dishes have been created around it. Before we get into three recipes using breasts of chicken stuffed with sausage, here are some interesting facts about suprêmes in general.*

*First of all, don't buy boneless breasts unless you are willing to pay a premium price for them. Boning a chicken breast is simplicity in itself. If you conquered boning out an entire chicken for Chicken Stuffed With Sausage and Czech Dressing, you can almost bone a breast with your eyes closed. Boning the breasts yourself has the added advantage of leaving you with a pile of bones for your stock pot.*

*Another little fact about suprêmes: the underside (bone side) of each breast has a little strip of flesh which runs along its length. This piece of flesh is called the fillet. It is to a chicken what a tenderloin is to a steer. And it is just as much a delicacy. Whenever you bone some chicken breasts, pull off this little strip (it comes off with gentle finger pressure). Freeze these fillets until you have some accumulated and then have a gourmet feast by sautéing them in a little clarified butter. Plan on at least a half a dozen per person, however, because they are very small.*

### First Recipe

**1 pound bulk fresh sausage (whatever you like best)**

**4 whole chicken breasts, boned, skinned, halved, and flattened**

**1 cup flour**

**2 eggs beaten with two tablespoons water**

**2 cups bread crumbs seasoned with the following: 1 teaspoon oregano, 1 teaspoon basil, 1 teaspoon parsley, 1 tablespoon Parmesan cheese, and 1 teaspoon freshly ground white pepper**

**Salt to taste, if desired**

**Oil for frying**

**1 teaspoon chopped fresh parsley**

**1 lemon, quartered**

1. Sauté the sausage until it is lightly browned, about ten minutes.

2. Dust each piece of breast with flour.

3. Place one quarter of the sausage meat on each of four breast halves. Leave a border all around the edges.

4. Place another breast half on top of each one with the sausage. (The chicken should be moist enough to make the flour adhere at the edges.)

5. Dip each combined breast into the egg wash and then coat with the seasoned bread crumbs. Press the crumbs in with the flat of your hand.

6. Heat the oil in a large skillet and sauté each breast until it is golden brown on both sides. Garnish with parsley and serve with a lemon wedge.

Serves 4.

## Second Recipe

2 whole chicken breasts,
boned, skinned, and halved
¼ pound hard salami, cut into
a quarter-inch dice
¼ pound shredded mozzarella
cheese
2 tablespoons *pignolia* (pine)
nuts, lightly toasted and
crushed
1 cup flour
2 eggs beaten with two tablespoons water
2 cups seasoned bread crumbs
(see preceding recipe)
Salt to taste, if desired
Oil for frying
Parsley for garnish

1. With a very sharp knife, cut a pocket in the plump side of each breast half. Be careful not to poke a hole through the side of the breast.

2. Mix the salami, mozzarella, and pine nuts. Divide the mixture into four equal portions and stuff the pocket of each breast.

3. Dust each breast with flour, dip in the egg wash, and coat with the seasoned crumbs.

4. Fry in hot oil until golden brown on each side. Garnish with parsley.

Serves 4.

## Third Recipe

2 whole chicken breasts,
boned, and halved
Salt to taste, if desired
Freshly ground black pepper
2 tablespoons clarified butter
¼ cup minced onion
¼ cup finely chopped
mushrooms
Dash of cayenne pepper
1 tablespoon chopped fresh
parsley
½ pound sweet Italian-style
sausage removed from the
casing and crumbled
4 teaspoons grated Romano
cheese
Oil for frying
4 cups tomato sauce
½ cup grated Parmesan cheese
1 tablespoon chopped fresh
parsley

1. Flatten each breast half and sprinkle with salt and pepper.

2. Heat the clarified butter in a skillet and sauté the onion and mushrooms until they are tender. Add a dash of cayenne and a tablespoon of parsley.

3. Mix the sautéed vegetables with the sausage meat and spread equal amounts on each breast half. Sprinkle the Romano cheese on each.

4. Roll up each breast, jelly roll fashion, and brown quickly in hot oil. The breasts should hold together as they cook, but you can secure each one with a toothpick to make them easier to handle.

5. Spread one cup of the tomato sauce on the bottom of a baking pan. Arrange the rollups in the pan and pour over the rest of the sauce. Sprinkle with Parmesan cheese.

6. Bake, covered, in a preheated 425° F oven for thirty minutes or until the breasts are tender. Garnish with parsley and serve.

Serves 4.

## Sausage and Chicken Sautéed in Red Wine Sauce

*This dish is a variation on a venerable French dish:* coq au vin.

¼ cup olive oil
1 three-pound broiler-fryer cut into serving pieces
1 pound fresh garlic sausage links
18 small new potatoes in their jackets
¼ cup minced celery
2 carrots, scraped, and cut into one-inch pieces
1 cup baby onions
2 cloves garlic, crushed
1 cup chicken stock
2 cups dry red wine
1 bay leaf
*Bouquet garni* (In a small square of cheesecloth, put one teaspoon thyme, one teaspoon marjoram, two sprigs of parsley and six peppercorns and tie the corners together with a string.
Salt to taste, if desired
Freshly ground black pepper

1. Heat the olive oil in the bottom of a Dutch oven and brown the chicken pieces, about twenty minutes. Remove with a slotted spoon and keep warm.

2. Brown the sausage in the Dutch oven, about twenty minutes. Remove and keep warm.

3. Add the potatoes, celery, carrots, onions, and garlic and sauté quickly until the vegetables are browned, about ten minutes.

4. Return the sausages and chicken to the pot. Add the chicken stock, wine, bay leaf, and *bouquet garni*. Bring to a simmer and cook, covered, for about one hour or until the chicken is tender. Remove the bay leaf and the *bouquet garni*.

Serves 4 to 6.

## Chicken Sausage Tandoori

*To be truly authentic, this dish would have to be cooked in a* tandoori *oven, but this recipe is nevertheless delicious.*

2 teaspoons ground coriander
4 teaspoons ground cumin seed
2 teaspoons cayenne
2 teaspoons sweet paprika
Salt to taste, if desired
Freshly ground black pepper
1 tablespoon finely minced gingeroot
3 cloves garlic, very finely minced
1 cup plain yogurt
2 pounds chicken sausage links

1. In a bowl, mix all the ingredients except the sausage.

2. Pour the mixture over the sausage, coating it well, and marinate in the refrigerator overnight.

3. Broil the sausage for about twenty minutes or until it is evenly browned and cooked through.

Serves 6.

# Sausage with Other Meats

Because sausage is so versatile, it can be combined with other meats to add flavor, to add a new twist to a new recipe, or simply to stretch a dish further in an economical fashion.

## Bracciole Stuffed with Sausage

Bracciole *is an Italian dish traditionally made from flank steak. It used to be that flank steaks weren't very popular and you could walk into a supermarket and cart one off for practically nothing. Now that you need an installment loan to buy meat, the flank has gone the way of the sirloin and the porterhouse. The problem is compounded by the fact that each steer comes equipped with only two small flank steaks. As more people find out what can be done with this piece of meat, the price will no doubt continue to climb. This dish can be prepared with thinly sliced round steak but the flavor won't be quite the same.*

1 one pound flank or bottom round steak
2 links hot Italian-style sausage
1 teaspoon coarsely ground fresh black pepper (lots of black pepper is one of the secrets of this dish)
¼ cup chopped Italian parsley
2 tablespoons grated Parmesan or Romano cheese
½ teaspoon crushed red pepper
1 clove garlic, minced
2 tablespoons chopped onion
½ teaspoon oregano
½ teaspoon basil
½ teaspoon chopped mint leaves
2 tablespoons vegetable oil
Tomato sauce

1. With the side of a meat cleaver or mallet, flatten the steak to a quarter-inch thickness. The meat should be rectangularly shaped.

2. Sprinkle all the herbs and spices and cheese evenly over the meat.

3. Place the sausages at the narrower end of the steak and roll it up jelly roll fashion. As you get towards the end, tuck the sides in.

4. With kitchen twine, tie the roll tightly at two-inch intervals.

5. Sauté the roll in the vegetable oil until it is browned on all sides.

6. Finish cooking in tomato sauce until tender, about ninety minutes. To serve cut into half-inch slices.

Serves 4 to 6.

## Boiled-Meats with Sausage

*Every cuisine has its own version of the boiled dinner: New England boiled dinner, the Italian* bolitto misto, *corned beef and cabbage. This recipe for a boiled dinner is a very hearty two-course meal, or it can be stretched into two meals, depending upon your requirements. The first course is a rich soup with Czech noodles called* polevka z drobečki *(literally soup with noodles). The second course consists of the meat which was simmered slowly to produce the soup along with a zesty tomato-based Czech gravy called* červena omačka *(literally red gravy).*

1 **two-pound beef brisket or lean blade chuck roast**
1 **small chicken with giblets**
5 **fresh link sausages, such as sweet Italian**
3 **carrots, scraped and cut into half-inch slices**
3 **stalks of celery, coarsely chopped**
3 **leaves of cabbage**
1 **large onion, studded with four cloves**
1 **stalk of Italian parsley**
*Bouquet garni* **(Czech style) consisting of 8 whole peppercorns, 2 bay leaves, ½ teaspoon thyme, ½ teaspoon basil, ½ teaspoon marjoram, and two whole allspice berries, tied in a cheesecloth bag**
**Water to cover**

**For the drobečki:**

2 **cups sifted all-purpose flour**
1 **egg, slightly beaten**
1 **teaspoon salt, or to taste**
1–2 **tablespoons water (approximately)**

**For the omačka:**

4 **tablespoons fat, skimmed from the broth**
4 **tablespoons flour**
1 **cup broth**
1 **cup tomato juice**
**Salt to taste, if desired**
**Freshly ground black pepper**

1. Place the beef, chicken, sausages, carrots, celery, cabbage leaves, onion, parsley, and *bouquet garni* in a large stock pot. Pour enough cold water into the pot to cover everything. Bring the pot to a boil and then reduce the heat so that the soup simmers gently. Skim off any scum that floats to the surface. Simmer for two hours.

2. While the stock is simmering, prepare the *drobečki* as follows: put the flour on a bread board and make a well in the center. Drop the egg into the well. Add the salt. With your fingers or a fork, begin mixing small amounts of flour into the egg. Add a small amount of water at a time. Work until you get a good stiff dough that can be formed into a ball. Knead the dough for a couple of minutes, wrap it in waxed paper, and refrigerate it until the soup is ready.

3. When the cooking time is up, remove the meats to a platter, slice, and keep warm. Strain the broth and return it to the pot.

4. Skim the fat from the soup, reserving four tablespoons and discard the rest. Place the four tablespoons of fat in a saucepan over medium heat. Blend in the flour, stirring constantly. When it begins to turn slightly brown, add the cup of broth and tomato juice, stirring until it bubbles and thickens. Pour the *omačka* into a bowl, cover, and keep warm.

5. Bring the remaining broth to a boil. Using the large holes of a food grater, grate the *drobečki* dough over a piece of waxed paper. Add these noodles to the boiling broth, a handful at a time, stirring. When all the noodles have been added, reduce the heat and simmer gently for five minutes.

6. Serve the soup as a first course and then serve the boiled meats with the gravy passed at the table.

Serves 6 to 8.

## Double Thick Pork Chops
## Stuffed with Sausage

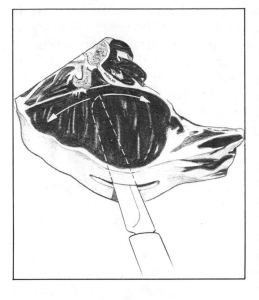

*There is only one way to stuff a pork chop so that the stuffing stays put. It's surprising how many people don't know how to do it.*

*The most common method of stuffing a pork chop is to slit it end to end opposite the bone. This is commonly called butterflying. When the chop is stuffed, skewered shut, and baked, however, the chop naturally shrinks and much of the filling leaks out.*

*For a much neater stuffed pork chop try this: with a very sharp pointed knife, pierce the chop in the center of the edge opposite the bone, then thrust the knife all the way to the bone. Without making that opening any larger, work a pocket into the chop by moving the knife first in one direction and then, turning it over, the other. Be careful not to poke a hole in the wall of the chop and to leave about a quarter-inch margin along the chop's outer edge. Fill the chop with stuffing by using a pastry tube or small funnel.*

**6 double thick (1½-inch) center-cut loin pork chops**
**¼ pound bulk country-style sausage**
**¼ cup diced bits of any cured sausage such as pepperoni, salami, etc.**
**1 tablespoon minced onion**
**1 teaspoon ground ginger root**
**½ cup dried bread crumbs**
**1 teaspoon chopped fresh parsley**
**2 tablespoons dry white wine**
**Salt to taste, if desired**
**Freshly ground black pepper**
**2 tablespoons olive oil**

1. Prepare the pockets in the chops.

2. Combine all the remaining ingredients except the oil and mix well. Stuff the chops.

3. Brush the chops with the oil, dust with salt and pepper, place on a broiling rack, and bake, uncovered, in a preheated 375° F oven for about forty-five minutes. Baste frequently with the pan juices to prevent the chops from drying out.

Serves 6.

## City Chicken Sausage Skewers

*There is a dish around these parts called "city chicken." Why or how it got to be called this I don't know because it isn't even remotely related to chicken. It consists of cubes of veal and pork alternately skewered on wooden skewers about six inches long. The skewers are floured, dipped in an egg wash, breaded, and fried.*

*This recipe is a variation on the city chicken theme. Substitute proportionate amounts of veal and pork cubes for the meat in this recipe if you would like to try the original.*

½ pound very lean finely
   ground bulk country sausage
½ pound lean ground veal
   seasoned with ¼ teaspoon
   minced garlic, 1 teaspoon
   minced onion, salt, and
   pepper to taste
Metal or wooden skewers
½ cup milk
½ cup flour
1 egg, beaten with two
   tablespoons water
1 cup seasoned bread crumbs
   (see recipe page 132)
Vegetable oil for frying

1. Divide the sausage and ground veal into equal portions to form one-inch meat balls.
2. String the sausage and veal ball onto the skewers, alternating them until all the meat is used.
3. Dip the skewered meat in the milk, dust with flour, and then dip into the egg wash, and finally into the seasoned bread crumbs. Place the skewers in the refrigerator for thirty minutes to set the coating.
4. Heat the oil in a large skillet and fry the city chicken sausage until it is golden on all sides.
5. Drain on paper toweling and then place them on a cookie sheet. Bake, uncovered, in a preheated 375° F oven for twenty minutes.

Serves 4.

## Hot Dogs Cooked in Beer

*Whether hot dogs cooked in beer are better because the beer adds something intrinsic to the meat, or simply because the vapors rising from the pot whet the appetite is a matter of conjecture. Suffice it to say that they are better.*

1 pound homemade hot dogs
1 12-ounce bottle beer or ale
1 cup water
2 cups sauerkraut, rinsed and
   drained
½ teaspoon caraway seed
Hot dog buns

1. Place the hot dogs in a pot with the beer and water. Bring to a boil and then reduce heat so that the liquid barely simmers. Cook for twenty minutes.
2. Place a colander or vegetable steamer over the pan with the hot dogs and place the sauerkraut in it. Sprinkle the caraway seed on the sauerkraut. Cover and allow the steam to heat the sauerkraut.
3. Make a bed of sauerkraut in each roll and place a dog on top. Instant picnic!

Serves 4.

# Fish Sausage with Orange Butter

*Citrus flavors meld well with seafood and this recipe is no exception.*

1 pound fish sausage
4 tablespoons clarified butter
2 tablespoons shallots, finely chopped
¼ cup orange liqueur
¼ cup orange juice
¼ cup heavy cream
1 tablespoon orange zest
Salt to taste, if desired
Freshly ground black pepper

1. Sauté the sausage in the butter until it is evenly browned and cooked through, about ten minutes. Remove and drain.

2. Sauté the shallots in the butter until soft, about five minutes.

3. Add the orange liqueur and juice. Cook over medium high heat until the mixture is reduced by half. Add the cream and continue to cook, stirring, until the mixture is slightly thickened, about three minutes.

4. Arrange the sausage on a platter and pour the sauce over all.

Serves 4.

# Fish Sausage Chili

*You can increase the "bite" of this dish by increasing the amount of cayenne pepper or adding some chopped fresh or tinned jalapeño peppers.*

¼ cup olive oil
2 large onions, coarsely chopped
1 cup chopped celery
¼ cup grated carrot
2 tablespoons garlic, minced
1 tablespoon oregano
1 28-ounce can crushed Italian-style tomatoes in puree
8 ounces bottled clam juice
2 cups dry red wine
1 tablespoon cumin seed
2 teaspoons cayenne pepper
Salt to taste, if desired
2 sweet green peppers, cored, seeded, and diced
2 pounds fish sausage

1. In the olive oil, in a Dutch oven, sauté the onion, celery, carrot, and garlic until slightly softened, about ten minutes.

2. Add the oregano, tomatoes, clam juice, wine, cumin, cayenne, and salt. Bring the mixture to a boil, reduce the heat, and simmer for thirty minutes.

3. Add the sweet pepper and simmer twenty minutes.

4. Add the sausage and simmer thirty minutes or until the sausage is cooked through.

Serves 6 to 8.

## Grilled Sausage with White Clam Sauce

*This dish has become a family tradition on warm summer evenings when something quick, light, and delicious is an absolute necessity. One ordinarily wouldn't think to combine clams and pork sausage, but this recipe proves that strange bedfellows can indeed be the best of friends, at least at the dinner table. Try this dish with a tossed green salad and cold beer or white sangria, and you'll become a lifelong devotee.*

2 pounds hot or sweet Italian-style sausage links
4 ounces (1 stick) butter
4 cloves garlic, minced
1 medium onion, coarsely chopped
1 cup chopped Italian parsley
2 6½-ounce cans chopped clams with their juice
Coarsely ground fresh black pepper (use a lot)
2 dozen fresh littleneck clams, scrubbed
1 pound linguine

1. Prepare a charcoal fire and begin grilling the sausages when the coals are covered by a grey ash. Plan on the sausages taking about forty-five minutes.

2. Start boiling a large kettle of water for cooking the pasta.

3. Melt the butter in a saucepan and add the garlic and onion. Sauté for about ten minutes or until the onion becomes translucent.

4. Add the parsley and the two cans of clams with their juice to the saucepan. Cook over medium heat for ten minutes. Add the black pepper.

5. Add the fresh clams, cover, and cook until the clams open.

(**Note:** make sure someone is tending the sausages while you are preparing the clam sauce.)

6. Cook the linguine. Drain. Spread it out on a large serving platter.

7. Pour the sauce over the linguine, arranging the whole clams on top and place the grilled sausages around the edges.

Serves 4 to 6.

## Sausage Spiedini

*Spiedini in Italian means "skewered." Other cultures variously call their skewered dishes kababs or shish kebabs, among other things, but by any name they are generally Mediterranean in origin. In this area we have a dish called spiedi (pronounced speedie) which is marinated cubes of lamb skewered and charcoal broiled. Various theories abound as to its exact origin, but the one that seems most plausible is that Italian shepherds, forced by circumstances to eat on the run, concocted the dish. The lambs they tended were now and then sacrified for a meal, the meat cubed and the herbs and spices which grew wild in abundance were pressed into the meat as much for preservation as for flavor. The cubes were skewered on saplings sticks and broiled over an open fire. Simple, but incredibly delicious! Future generations brought variations of the dish to this country. The name* spiedi *is an Americanization of* spiedini.

*Combinations of meat and vegetables for kebabs or* spiedini *are limited only by one's imagination, but certain combinations by their very nature suggest themselves as perfect culinary marriages. Italian sausages, small onions, green peppers, and mushrooms are perfect go-togethers. Experiment with your own combinations.*

**1 pound hot or sweet Italian-style sausage cut into one-inch pieces**
**24 (approximately) one-inch onions, peeled**
**24 (approximately) square pieces of green pepper**
**24 (approximately) fresh mushroom caps**
**½ cup olive oil**
**¼ cup lemon juice**
**1 teaspoon oregano**
**1 teaspoon basil**
**½ teaspoon crushed red pepper**
**1 teaspoon rosemary**
**½ teaspoon crushed mint leaves**
**1 clove garlic, finely minced**
**Salt to taste, if desired**
**Freshly ground black pepper**

1. Put the sausage, onions, pepper squares, and mushrooms in a bowl. Pour on the oil and lemon juice and add the remaining ingredients. Mix well.

2. Marinate overnight in the refrigerator.

3. Alternate pieces of sausage and vegetables on long metal skewers. Reserve the marinade.

4. Broil the *spiedini* over a hot charcoal fire until the sausage is cooked through. Baste frequently with the reserved marinade to prevent the vegetables from burning before the sausage is cooked.

## Sausage Spiedini with Veal

*Although wooden skewers will work with this recipe if they are first soaked in water, metal skewers are the best choice.*

**1 pound hot or sweet Italian-style sausage cut into one-inch pieces**
**1 pound veal cubes cut into one-inch pieces**
**Marinade (see previous recipe)**

1. Combine the sausage and veal pieces with the marinade ingredients and marinate overnight.

2. Skewer alternating pieces of sausage and veal, and charcoal broil, basting frequently, until the meat is done.

Serves 4 to 6.

## Veal Oreganato with Sausage

*I am indebted to my good friend, Vince Luizzi, for the idea for this recipe.*

1 tablespoon olive oil
8 quarter-inch thick veal cutlets, about two pounds
8 sweet Italian-style sausage links
4 potatoes, peeled and cut into two-inch pieces
2 sweet green peppers, cored, seeded, and cut into one-inch strips
½ cup chopped onion
2 cloves garlic, finely minced
3 cups tomato sauce
1 cup dry white wine
1½ teaspoons crushed oregano
1 tablespoon chopped parsley
Salt and pepper to taste
1 tablespoon olive oil

1. Grease a baking pan with one tablespoon of the olive oil. Spread one cup of the tomato sauce evenly in the pan. Arrange the veal, sausages, potatoes, and peppers in the pan. Add the onion and garlic.
2. Pour the rest of the tomato sauce and the wine over all.
3. Sprinkle the remaining ingredients evenly over all.
4. Bake, uncovered, in a preheated 375° F oven for about one hour or until all the meats are tender. Place the meats and potatoes on a platter and pass the pan sauce at the table.
Serves 6 to 8.

## Sausage Stuffed Meat Loaf

*This special meat loaf contains a surprise in the center.*

2 links fresh sausage (your favorite variety)
½ pound lean ground beef
½ pound lean ground pork
½ pound lean ground veal
1½ cups soft bread crumbs
2 eggs well beaten
½ teaspoon oregano
½ teaspoon basil
¼ cup finely chopped onion
½ teaspoon crushed mint leaves
1 clove garlic, finely minced
⅛ teaspoon nutmeg
2 tablespoons chopped parsley
¼ cup grated Romano cheese
½ cup dry red wine
2 shelled hard-boiled eggs
1 cup tomato sauce
¼ cup grated Parmesan cheese
Salt and pepper to taste

1. Parboil the sausage links in enough water to cover for fifteen minutes. Remove and drain.
2. In a large mixing bowl, combine the ground meats, bread crumbs, eggs, oregano, basil, onion, mint, garlic, nutmeg, parsley, Romano cheese, and wine. Mix well.
3. Turn half the meat mixture into a greased loaf pan, pressing it down firmly. Arrange the sausage links and hard-boiled eggs in the center of the meat. Press more meat in between them, and then cover with the remaining meat, pressing it down firmly to seal.
4. Bake, uncovered, in a preheated 425° F oven for forty-five minutes. Remove from the oven, and spread the tomato sauce over the meat loaf and sprinkle on the Parmesan cheese. Return it to the oven for twenty minutes. Allow the meat loaf to stand at room temperature for about ten minutes before carving.
Serves 4 to 6.

# Sausage with Vegetables: Soups, Stews, and Casseroles

Nowhere is sausage's versatility more evident than in the multitude of ways in which it can be combined with fresh vegetables.

## Cassoulet

*Cassoulet is a French casserole. Traditional versions usually use goose or duck fat, but the dish can be successfully made using vegetable oil with only a minor sacrifice in flavor but without the added cholesterol. Although duck and/or goose are also traditional ingredients, chicken, which is much leaner, is a worthy substitute.*

1 3—4 pound chicken
Salt to taste, if desired
Freshly ground black pepper
1 small onion, studded with four cloves
2 cloves garlic, peeled and crushed
½ pound lean ground pork
½ pound lean ground lamb
1 pound fresh garlic or Polish sausage
2 large sweet onions, peeled, and thinly sliced
2 cloves of garlic, finely minced
1 cup finely chopped celery with tops
1 cup thinly sliced carrots
2 15-ounce cans navy beans
1 cup dry white wine
1 cup tomato juice
1 tablespoon tomato paste
½ teaspoon thyme leaves
1 bay leaf
2 tablespoons chopped parsley

1. Rub the chicken inside and out with salt and pepper. Insert the onion and the two cloves of garlic into the bird's cavity. Roast on a rack in a preheated 375° F oven until done (about 1 hour). Cool, remove the meat from the bone, and cut it into serving pieces.

2. In a Dutch oven, sauté the ground pork and lamb until it is lightly browned. Remove it with a slotted spoon and sit it aside. Sauté the sausage in the Dutch oven until it is well browned. Remove and set aside.

3. Sauté the onions, garlic, celery, and carrots until they are crisp-tender, about five minutes. Drain off as much accumulated fat as possible.

4. Add the beans with their juice, wine, tomato juice, tomato paste, thyme, bay leaf, and the chopped parsley. Return the ground meat and sausage to the pot and bring to a simmer.

5. Add the pieces of chicken and simmer for fifteen minutes.

6. Transfer the mixture to a large casserole and cook, uncovered, in a preheated 375° F oven for forty-five minutes. Remove the bay leaf before serving.

Serves 8 to 10.

## Acorn Squash Stuffed with Sausage

*This is virtually a complete meal in one dish. A tossed salad is about all that is needed to complete the fixin's.*

2 large acorn squash
2 teaspoons brown sugar
1 pound bulk pork sausage
½ cup bread crumbs
1 egg, well beaten

1. Cut each squash in half and scrape out the seeds and pith.

2. Sprinkle the cavity of each squash with half a teaspoon of brown sugar.

3. Pour a small amount of water in the bottom of a baking pan, put in the squash and bake, uncovered, in a preheated 375° F oven for twenty minutes.

4. Meanwhile combine the sausage, bread crumbs, and egg. Mix well.

5. At the end of the twenty minutes, remove the squash from the oven and stuff one quarter of the sausage mixture into each of the squash halves.

6. Return the squash to the oven and continue to bake for thirty minutes or until the sausage is cooked through and crisp on top.

Serves 4.


## Beef and Sausage Stew

*Stew is always a heartwarmer on a cold blustery day and the addition of sausage in this recipe makes it even more so.*

2 tablespoons vegetable oil
1 pound beef stew meat, cut into one-inch cubes
1 pound link pork sausage
2 cups beef broth
2 cups tomato sauce
½ cup dry red wine
2 large potatoes, peeled and cubed
2 carrots, scraped and sliced
1 cup green peas (fresh or frozen)
1 cup tiny white onions, peeled
1 tablespoon chopped parsley
Salt to taste, if desired
Freshly ground black pepper

1. Heat the oil in a Dutch oven and sauté the beef cubes and sausages until they are browned.

2. Add the beef broth, tomato sauce, and wine and simmer gently, covered, for one hour.

3. Add the remaining ingredients and simmer until the vegetables are tender, about thirty minutes.

Serves 4 to 6.

## Bratwurst with German Potato Salad

*German potato salad derives its distinctive flavor from bits of crisp-fried bacon and some of the grease from that bacon. This recipe is just as flavorful, if not more so, and probably somewhat more healthful, too, since vegetable oil is used to cook the sausage.*

3 tablespoons vegetable oil
1 pound bratwurst
6 large potatoes, peeled, boiled, and sliced
1 large onion, peeled and thinly sliced
¼ cup cider vinegar
Salt to taste, if desired
Freshly ground coarse black pepper

1. Sauté the bratwurst in the vegetable oil until they are browned and cooked through, about twenty minutes. Set aside and keep warm.
2. In a large serving bowl, mix the potatoes and onions.
3. Slice the bratwurst into bite-sized pieces and add to the potatoes and onions. Add two tablespoons of oil from the sausage pan.
4. Add the vinegar, salt, and pepper. Mix well and taste for seasoning. May be served warm or cold.
Serves 4.

## Bubble and Squeak

*Bubble and Squeak is an old-time English dish traditionally made with beef and cabbage. This recipe uses sausage meat instead.*

1 small head cabbage (about two pounds)
1 pound bulk sausage meat
2 tablespoons clarified butter
2 tablespoons flour
1 cup milk
1 small onion, thinly sliced
1 clove garlic, finely minced
2 teaspoons Worcestershire sauce
Salt to taste, if desired
Freshly ground black pepper

1. Cut the cabbage into quarters and boil it in water until tender. Drain, chop finely, and set aside.
2. Break up the sausage and sauté it in a skillet until it is lightly browned. Remove it with a slotted spoon and set it aside. Discard all but one tablespoon of the drippings.
3. Add the clarified butter to the skillet and over medium heat, gradually add the flour, stirring constantly, until the mixture is smooth.
4. Add the milk and continue stirring until the mixture thickens.
5. Add the garlic, onion, sausage, cabbage, Worcestershire sauce, salt, and pepper. Mix well.
6. Place the mixture in a lightly greased casserole and bake, uncovered, in a preheated 325° F oven until the sauce is bubbly, about thirty minutes.
Serves 4.

## Choucroute

*Choucroute is French for sauerkraut, but it doesn't begin to describe everything that goes into this dish to make it a hearty and delicious repast for a cold winter's evening. It is a showcase for a variety of your homemade sausages.*

2 tablespoons vegetable oil
1 large onion, thinly sliced
1 small rack of pork spareribs (about two pounds) cut into serving pieces of one to two ribs each
4 small lean smoked loin pork chops
1 quart sauerkraut, rinsed and drained
4 cups shredded cabbage
2 cloves garlic, crushed
1 bay leaf
½ teaspoon ground cloves
2 cups (approximately) dry white wine
1–1½ pounds any assorted combination of the following sausages: kielbasa, Italian, knockwurst, bratwurst, thuringer or hot dogs

1. Heat the oil in a large, heavy skillet and sauté the onion until it is translucent. Remove with a slotted spoon and set aside.

2. Add the spareribs to the skillet and brown them quickly over medium high heat.

3. Return the onion to the pot. Add all the remaining ingredients except the sausages. Pour in enough wine to cover everything.

4. Cover and simmer this mixture for two hours *or* put everything in a large casserole and place, covered, in a preheated 325° F oven for two and a half hours. Check frequently and add more wine if necessary.

5. At the end of the cooking time, add the sausages and cook, covered, for an additional thirty minutes or until the sausages are done.

Serves 4.

## Creamed Broccoli with Summer Sausage

*A member of the cabbage family, broccoli was first cultivated in Italy over four hundred years ago. It is rich in vitamins and minerals and, with the protein from the milk, cheese and sausage, it makes a very nutritious meal.*

1½ pounds fresh broccoli
1 cup milk
2 cups grated sharp Cheddar cheese
1 cup diced summer sausage
1 tablespoon butter or margarine
Salt to taste, if desired
Freshly ground black pepper

1. Prepare the broccoli. Wash, trim, and cut into florets. Steam eight to ten minutes or until it is crisp-tender. Place the broccoli in a two-quart casserole.

2. In a saucepan, heat the milk and stir in the grated cheese. Cook, stirring, until the cheese is melted. Add the sausage.

3. Pour the sauce over the broccoli, dot with butter or margarine and bake, uncovered, in a preheated 375° F oven for fifteen minutes or until the cheese sauce is bubbly.

Serves 4.

## Eggplant Parmesan

*You may bread the eggplant before frying it, but if you're concerned about the calories, it is just as delicious without the breading.*

1 medium eggplant
1 cup flour seasoned with salt and pepper
¼ cup vegetable oil
1 pound sweet Italian-style sausage
4 cups tomato sauce
12 ounces grated mozzarella cheese
¼ cup grated Parmesan cheese
1 tablespoon olive oil

1. Prepare the eggplant. Wash, dry, and cut into quarter-inch thick slices.

2. Dust the slices with the seasoned flour.

3. Heat the vegetable oil in a large skillet and sauté the eggplant, a few slices at a time, until they are golden. Drain on paper toweling and set aside.

4. Sauté the sausage in the skillet until it is lightly browned. Remove it with a slotted spoon and set it aside.

5. Spread a thin layer of tomato sauce over the bottom of a baking pan. Arrange about half the eggplant slices over the sauce. Layer half the sausage over the eggplant followed by half the mozzarella and Parmesan cheeses. Add another layer of sauce and repeat the layering process. End with a layer of sauce. Dribble the olive oil over the top.

6. Bake, covered, in a preheated 375° F oven for thirty minutes. Remove the cover and bake an additional thirty minutes.

Serves 4 to 6.

## Kielbasa with Green Beans and Carrots

*Plan on having some fresh crusty bread on hand when you make this dish to sop up the delicious juices.*

1 pound fresh kielbasa cut into one-inch pieces
1 small onion, thinly sliced
1 cup dry white wine
2 cups water
2 cups Romano (Italian) green beans, cut into one-inch pieces
2 cups carrots, scraped and sliced
1 bay leaf
2 tablespoons chopped parsley
1 teaspoon paprika
Salt to taste, if desired
Freshly ground black pepper

1. Put the kielbasa into a Dutch oven with just enough water to cover the bottom. Cook over medium heat until the sausage is lightly browned and the water has evaporated, about fifteen minutes. Drain off the fat.

2. Add the onion and cook, over medium low heat, until the onion is translucent.

3. Add the remaining ingredients and cook about thirty minutes or until the vegetables are tender. Remove the bay leaf before serving.

Serves 4.

# Holupki

Holupki *is a dish of Slavic origin which consists of cabbage leaves stuffed, rolled, and baked in a tomato sauce. They are traditional at Eastertime. This recipe is my mother's. She makes it in voluminous quantities at Easter, but with the proportions here, you should be able to enjoy it at any time.*

1 head cabbage
2 tablespoons vegetable oil
1 medium onion, chopped
1 cup cooked rice
1½ pounds sausage stuffing
   (1 pound ground lean beef,
   ½ pound ground lean pork,
   1½ teaspoons salt, 1
   teaspoon ground black
   pepper)
5 cups tomato puree

1. Core the cabbage and place it in a large pot of rapidly boiling water. Boil until the cabbage leaves begin to fall away from each other. Remove and set aside until cool enough to handle.

2. In a skillet, sauté the onion in the vegetable oil, about five minutes.

3. Cook the rice according to package directions.

4. Mix together the rice, onion, and sausage meat.

5. Pull apart the cabbage leaves. Cut out the tough center stem of each one.

6. Place about a quarter cup of the sausage and rice stuffing mixture on one end of a leaf and roll it up, tucking in the sides to enclose the stuffing. Repeat until all the ingredients are used.

7. Place the *holupki* in a single layer in a roasting pan. Pour the tomato puree over all.

8. Bake covered, for one hour and fifteen minutes in a preheated 375° F oven.

Serves 4 to 6.

# Capusta

*In Polish,* capusta *means cabbage.*

2 tablespoons vegetable oil
1 large onion, peeled and
   chopped
1 pound smoked kielbasa, cut
   into one-inch pieces
1 small head of cabbage,
   shredded
1 cup tomato juice
Salt to taste, if desired
Freshly ground black pepper

1. Heat the oil in a Dutch oven and sauté the onion until it is translucent, about ten minutes.

2. Add the kielbasa and sauté for five minutes.

3. Add the remaining ingredients, cover, and cook for one hour at a bare simmer. Serve with rye bread or over boiled potatoes.

Serves 4.

# Leek and Sausage Casserole

*Use whatever variety of bulk sausage you like best in this recipe.*

1 pound bulk sausage
10 medium leeks
1 cup grated Swiss or Cheddar
  cheese
Dash of cayenne pepper
Salt to taste, if desired
Freshly ground black pepper

1. Crumble the sausage in a skillet and cook until lightly browned. Remove it with a slotted spoon.

2. Prepare the leeks. Cut off the green tops to within two inches of the white part. Wash well and steam until crisp-tender, about ten minutes.

3. Arrange the leeks in the bottom of a lightly greased baking dish. Layer the cooked sausage on top of the leeks. Sprinkle on the grated cheese, cayenne, salt, and pepper.

4. Place under a preheated broiler for about five minutes or until the cheese is bubbly and lightly browned.

Serves 4.

# Minestrone

*The sausage in this recipe adds flavor and richness to the stock of the Italian soup.*

2 tablespoons olive oil
1 pound sweet Italian-style
  sausage links, cut into one-
  inch pieces
2 carrots, scraped and cut into
  quarter-inch slices
2 celery stalks, cut into quarter-
  inch slices
1 small zucchini, sliced
1 medium onion, chopped
2 cloves garlic, minced
4 tomatoes, peeled, cored,
  seeded, and chopped
½ teaspoon thyme
½ teaspoon sage
Water
1 cup green beans
1 small can chick peas with
  their liquid
1 cup small macaroni shells
Salt to taste, if desired
Freshly ground black pepper
1 tablespoon chopped fresh
  parsley
Parmesan cheese, grated

1. Heat the olive oil in a Dutch oven and brown the sausage.

2. Add the carrots, celery, zucchini, onion, garlic, tomatoes, thyme, and sage. Bring to a simmer. Add about three quarts of cold water, bring to a boil, reduce heat, and simmer, uncovered, for two hours.

3. Add the green peas, chick peas with their liquid, macaroni, salt, and pepper. Simmer an additional ten minutes or until the macaroni is tender. Stir in the parsley. Serve hot with the Parmesan cheese to pass.

Serves 4 to 6.

## Paella

*Paella is a Spanish rice dish for company. Your home-made chorizos give this recipe a solid foundation.*

1 two-pound lobster
½ cup olive oil
2 three-pound frying chickens
3 cloves garlic, finely minced
1 large chopped onion
1 pound chorizos, cut into one-inch pieces
1 cup diced smoked ham
1 sweet green pepper, cored, seeded, and chopped
1 teaspoon capers (the brined, not salted variety)
2 cups crushed tomatoes
2 cups uncooked rice
1 big pinch saffron
1 cup water
1 small jar pimientos
1 teaspoon oregano
1 teaspoon ground coriander
Dash of cayenne pepper
1 pound cooked shrimp
1–2 dozen fresh clams, well scrubbed and steamed
1 cup fresh or frozen peas, cooked

If you can, in good conscience, afford all these ingredients, then there we go.

1. Boil or steam the lobster for fifteen minutes. When the lobster is cool enough to handle, remove the meat from the shell.

2. Cut the frying chicken into serving pieces and sauté in the olive oil until it is browned.

3. Add the garlic, onion, chorizos, ham, pepper, and capers to the pot with the chicken. Cook ten minutes, stirring.

4. Add the tomatoes, rice, saffron, water, pimientos, oregano, coriander, and cayenne. Mix well and cook, covered, twenty minutes or until the liquid is absorbed by the rice. Add the shrimp, lobster, clams, and peas. Heat through and serve.

Serves 8.

## Sausage and Bean Casserole

*In addition to being delicious, this dish is quick and easy to fix.*

2 16-ounce cans pork and bean in tomato sauce
1 small onion, chopped
1 sweet green pepper, cored, seeded, and chopped
¼ cup ketchup
2 tablespoons prepared mustard
1 pound homemade sausage links (any variety)

1. Mix together the first five ingredients.

2. Cut up the sausage into one-inch pieces and stir into the bean mixture.

3. Bake, covered, in a preheated 375° F oven for about one hour.

Serves 4.

## Sausage and Corn One-Dish Supper

*Creamed corn casserole is a good old fashioned addition to any meal. The casserole becomes almost the entire meal with the addition of sausage.*

1 tablespoon vegetable oil
1 pound country-style sausage
4 tablespoons butter or
   margarine
¼ cup chopped onion
¼ cup flour
2 cups milk
4 cups fresh or frozen corn
   parboiled for five minutes
1 sweet green pepper, cored,
   seeded, and coarsely chopped
¼ cup chopped fresh jalapeño
   peppers (optional)
¼ cup chopped pimiento
Salt to taste, if desired
Freshly ground black pepper
1½ cups cracker crumbs

1. Cut the sausage into one-inch pieces and brown in the vegetable oil in a large skillet. Remove with a slotted spoon. Drain off the grease.

2. Melt the butter in the skillet and sauté the onion until it is translucent.

3. Add the flour and milk, and cook, stirring, for five minutes.

4. Return the sausage to the skillet and add the corn, peppers, pimiento, salt, and pepper. Mix well.

5. Layer a greased casserole with one third of the cracker crumbs and top with one third of the sausage and corn mixture. Repeat layering twice, ending with a layer of crumbs.

6. Bake, uncovered, in a preheated 350° F oven for twenty minutes or until the casserole is bubbly and browned on top.

Serves 4.

## Sausage and Lentils

*The lentil is the dried seed of a plant from the pea family. Dried peas could, in fact, be substituted in this recipe.*

1 pound Polish or other fresh
   sausage, cut into one-inch
   pieces
1 large sweet onion, thinly
   sliced
1 teaspoon crushed mint leaves
6 cups water
1 cup dry white wine
2 cups dry lentils
1 teaspoon lemon or orange
   zest
1 tablespoon chopped parsley
1 tablespoon tomato paste
Salt to taste, if desired
Freshly ground black pepper

1. In a Dutch oven, brown the sausage pieces lightly. Start with a little water to get the juice from the sausages flowing.

2. Add the onion and cook five minutes.

3. Add the remaining ingredients, bring to a boil. Reduce heat and simmer forty-five minutes, covered.

Serves 4.

## Dandelions and Sausage

*One of the first harbingers of spring, dandelions, are delicious when prepared with sweet Italian sausage.*

2 tablespoons olive oil
1 pound sweet Italian-style sausage, cut into one-inch pieces
2 pounds fresh dandelion greens
¼ cup tomato sauce
Grated Parmesan cheese
Salt to taste, if desired
Freshly ground black pepper

1. Heat the oil in a Dutch oven and sauté the sausage until it is well browned. Remove with a slotted spoon.
2. Wash the greens and drain. Add them to the Dutch oven and cook, covered, over medium low heat until they are tender, about fifteen minutes.
3. Return the sausage to the pot and add the remaining ingredients. Heat through and serve.

Serves 4 as a side dish.

## Sausage and Peas with Tomato Sauce

*This is a perfect late spring or early summer dish, when the peas are ready and the first tender leaves of mint and basil are ready for the plucking.*

2 tablespoons vegetable oil
1 pound sweet Italian-style sausage, cut into one-inch pieces
3 cups ditalini macaroni
2 cups shelled fresh or frozen peas
3 cups tomato sauce
1 teaspoon crushed mint leaves
3 fresh basil leaves
Salt to taste, if desired
Freshly ground black pepper
1 tablespoon chopped fresh parsley

1. Heat the oil in a heavy skillet and brown the sausages. Drain off the fat.
2. Cook the macaroni according to package directions.
3. Steam the peas until crisp-tender, about five minutes.
4. Add the remaining ingredients, except the parsley, and bring to a simmer for ten minutes.
5. Add the drained, cooked macaroni, heat through and serve.

Serves 4.

## Sausage and Vegetable Curry

*Most Indian cooks have their own special recipe for curry powder and if you feel adventurous, you might want to experiment with your own combinations of spices. The premixed variety on your grocer's shelf works just as well with this recipe.*

3 tablespoons vegetable or
  peanut oil
2 pounds fresh sausage links,
  cut into one-inch pieces
1 small onion, chopped
1 carrot, scraped and thinly
  sliced
4 cups fresh green beans, cut
  into one-inch pieces
1 teaspoon red pepper flakes
2 teaspoons curry powder
Buttered rice

1. Heat the oil in a large skillet and brown the sausage pieces. Drain off all but two tablespoons of fat.
2. Add the carrot and onion and sauté until crisp-tender.
3. Add the remaining ingredients except the rice and cook, stirring, over medium heat ten minutes or until the beans are crisp-tender. Serve over hot buttered rice.

Serves 4.

## Sausage Goulash

*Use any mildly spiced German, French or Italian sausage for this recipe.*

2 tablespoons vegetable oil
1 pound fresh sausage links,
  cut into one-inch pieces
2 large sweet onions, very
  thinly sliced
2 cloves garlic, crushed
4 cups water
2 tablespoons sweet paprika
1 tablespoon chopped fresh
  parsley
Salt to taste, if desired
Freshly ground black pepper
Cooked rice or rye bread

1. Heat the oil in a Dutch oven and sauté the sausage until it is browned. Remove the meat and keep warm.
2. Sauté the onion and garlic until the onion is translucent, about ten minutes.
3. Put the meat back in the pot, add the water, paprika, parsley, salt, and pepper. Simmer gently for thirty minutes. Serve hot over rice or with rye bread.

Serves 4.

## Sausage Hash

*The word, hash, has evil connotations for many people because it conjurs up thoughts of leftovers that should have been left to rest. There is nothing leftover about this recipe. Vary the flavor by using any variety of fresh sausage.*

4 cups (about 1½ pounds)
   fresh bulk sausage
½ cup chopped onion
4 cups peeled, cooked, and
   chopped potatoes
½ cup cooked, chopped carrots
Vegetable oil

1. Sauté the sausage until it is lightly browned. Remove with a slotted spoon.
2. Sauté the onion in the sausage drippings until it is translucent, about ten minutes. Drain off as much fat as possible.
3. Return the sausage to the skillet and add the potatoes and carrots. Mix well.
4. Place the mixture in a bowl and wipe out the skillet. Add the vegetable oil to the skillet and heat. Form the hash into patties and fry until browned on both sides.
Serves 4.

## Sausage Paprikash

Paprikash *means "made with paprika." Unfortunately the paprika to which many Americans are accustomed is nothing at all like the real thing. True Hungarian paprika comes in a spectrum of flavors ranging from mild and sweet to extremely pungent. One thing that all Hungarian varieties have in common and the thing that most domestic varieties lack, is flavor. Many people consequently think of paprika as basically a coloring agent when it should be considered as a flavoring agent.*

2 tablespoons vegetable oil
2 pounds kielbasa or other
   fresh sausage, cut into one-
   inch pieces
2 large sweet onions, peeled,
   quartered, and thinly sliced
4 cups beef or veal stock,
   preferrably homemade
1 12-ounce can beer or ale
3 tablespoons paprika
½ cup chopped parsley
Salt to taste, if desired
Freshly ground black pepper
¼ cup flour
Buttered noodles

1. Heat the vegetable oil in a Dutch oven and sauté the sausage until it browned. Drain off the accumulated fat.
2. Add the onion, stock, beer, and paprika. Bring to a boil, reduce heat, and simmer, uncovered, for thirty minutes.
3. Add salt and pepper to taste.
4. Add enough cold water to the flour to make a thin paste and add this to the simmering liquid, stirring constantly, until the mixture thickens.
5. Add the parsley. Serve over hot buttered noodles.
Serves 4.

## Sausage with Onions, Peppers, and Mushrooms in Wine Sauce

*This recipe makes an excellent buffet dish for a party. It is easy and quick to prepare and can be scooped into party rolls to be eaten out of hand.*

2 pounds hot or sweet Italian-style sausage
2 tablespoons olive oil
2 large sweet onions, sliced thinly
2 large red or green sweet peppers, cored, seeded, and cut into strips
1 pound fresh mushrooms, sliced thinly
1 cup dry white wine

1. In a large skillet, sauté the sausage in the olive oil until it is well browned. Remove it with a slotted spoon and set it aside.

2. In the same skillet, sauté the onions and peppers until they are crisp-tender. Remove them with a slotted spoon and set them aside.

3. Sauté the mushrooms until they give up most of their liquid. Drain the fat from the skillet.

4. Cut the sausage into half-inch thick slices and return it to the skillet along with the onions and peppers.

5. Add the wine and cook over medium heat until the liquid is almost evaporated.

Serves 4 to 6.

## Scalloped Potatoes with Sausage

*Any spicy fresh sausage works well in this recipe.*

1 pound fresh sausage links
6 large potatoes
3 tablespoons butter or margarine
2 tablespoons flour
3 cups milk
Dash of cayenne pepper
Salt to taste, if desired
Freshly ground black pepper
1 onion, sliced thinly

1. In a skillet, cook the sausage in just enough water to cover the bottom of the pan. When it is lightly browned, remove it and set it aside until it is cool enough to handle. Cut it into half-inch thick slices.

2. Scrub and peel the potatoes. Slice them thinly.

3. In a saucepan, melt the butter and mix in the flour to make a *roux*. Add the milk, a little at a time, stirring, until the mixture thickens. Add the cayenne, salt, and pepper to taste.

4. In a lightly greased casserole, layer the potatoes, onion, sausage, and sauce. Begin and end with a layer of sauce.

5. Bake, covered, in a preheated 425° F oven for forty minutes. Uncover and bake an additional twenty minutes to brown.

Serves 4.

## Spanish Rice with Chorizos

*Most Spanish rice recipes call for browned ground beef, but the addition of chorizos gives this recipe more flavor.*

2 slices diced bacon
2 tablespoons vegetable oil
1 pound fresh chorizo
  sausages, cut into one-inch
  pieces
1 medium onion, chopped
1 sweet green pepper, seeded,
  cored, and chopped
2 cups tomato sauce
1 cup uncooked rice
Salt to taste, if desired
Freshly ground black pepper

1. Cook the bacon until it is crisp. Remove it with a slotted spoon and drain it on paper towels. Drain off the fat from the skillet.

2. Heat the vegetable oil in the skillet and sauté the chorizos until they are browned. Remove with a slotted spoon. Drain off all but two tablespoons of fat.

3. Sauté the onions and peppers until they are crisp-tender.

4. Return the bacon and chorizos to the skillet, add the tomato sauce and bring to a simmer.

5. Cook the rice according to package directions.

6. Add the rice to the skillet, mix well, add salt and pepper and serve warm.

Serves 4.

## Spanish Sausage Soup

*This soup is hearty enough to be the main event at dinner on a cold winter's night.*

2 tablespoons vegetable oil
1 pound fresh chorizos, cut
  into one-inch pieces
2 large potatoes, peeled and
  diced
1 carrot, scraped and sliced
1 celery stalk, with top,
  chopped coarsely
1 large onion, chopped
1 10-ounce package frozen
  baby lima beans
2 quarts chicken or beef stock,
  preferably homemade
2 tablespoons tomato paste
Salt to taste, if desired
Freshly ground black pepper

1. Heat the oil in a Dutch oven and sauté the sausage until it is well browned.

2. Add the potatoes, carrot, celery, and onion to the pot and sauté about five minutes. Drain off as much fat as possible.

3. Add the lima beans, stock, tomato paste, salt, and pepper. Simmer, uncovered for forty-five minutes. Serve hot.

Serves 4 to 6.

# Stir Fried Sausage and Vegetables

*This Chinese-style dish is extremely nutritious and can be prepared quickly.*

1½ tablespoons peanut or vegetable oil

2 cloves garlic, crushed

2 teaspoons freshly ground ginger

1 pound mild pork sausage, links, cut into one-inch pieces

4 carrots, scraped and thinly sliced

2 sweet red or green peppers, cored, seeded, and cut into strips

4 green onions, cut into half-inch pieces

3 cups coarsely shredded cabbage

1 cup sliced celery


**Optional ingredients:**

Bean sprouts
Fresh mushrooms
Bamboo shoots
Water chestnuts
Fresh spinach
Fresh broccoli
Fresh cauliflower
1 tablespoon cornstarch
2 tablespoons soy sauce (may be low sodium variety)
2 tablespoons Worcestershire sauce
Cooked rice

1. Heat the oil in a large heavy skillet or a wok. Add the garlic and sauté until it is lightly browned. Remove it. Add the ginger and the sausage. Cook until the sausage is browned. Remove the sausage with a slotted spoon. Keep it warm. Drain off all but two tablespoons of fat.

2. Add the vegetables and over high heat, stir constantly. Add the vegetables in order of *descending* time needed to cook.

3. Return the sausage to the skillet.

4. Combine the cornstarch with the soy sauce and Worcestershire sauce and pour this mixture into the skillet. Cook over high heat, stirring constantly, until the sauce thickens and the vegetables are well coated. Serve over rice.

Serves 4 to 6.

## Swedish Meatballs and Sausage

*Every good cook has a Swedish meatball recipe in his or her repertoire. This should prove an interesting variation for even the most discriminating of tastes.*

1 ring Swedish sausage (*Potatis Korv*)
2 tablespoons vegetable oil
½ cup finely chopped onion
½ pound lean ground beef
½ pound lean ground pork
½ pound lean ground veal
1 cup fresh bread crumbs
1 clove garlic, very finely minced
⅛ teaspoon nutmeg
⅛ teaspoon allspice
2 eggs, well beaten
Salt to taste, if desired
Freshly ground black pepper
Vegetable oil for frying
1 10½-ounce can cream of mushroom soup
½ cup dry white wine
½ cup water

1. Boil the sausage in a large pot for forty minutes. Remove, pat dry, and set it aside.
2. Assemble the meatballs by sautéing the chopped onion in the vegetable oil until it is translucent. Remove it with a slotted spoon and combine it with the beef, pork, veal, bread crumbs, garlic, nutmeg, allspice, eggs, salt, and pepper. Mix well and shape into one-inch meatballs.
3. Sauté the meatballs in vegetable oil until they are browned. Remove with a slotted spoon and set aside.
4. Slice the sausage into bite-sized pieces and sauté it in the same skillet used for the meatballs until it is browned. Drain off as much fat as possible.
5. Return the meatballs to the skillet. Add the mushroom soup, wine, and water. Cook over medium heat, stirring, until the mixture bubbles.

Serves 4 to 6.

## Texas-Style Sausage Chili

*You can either use bulk country-style sausage or fresh chorizos in this recipe.*

1 pound bulk sausage
2 cloves garlic, minced
1 medium onion, chopped
3 tablespoons chili powder (or substitute your own combination of spices such as ground chilis, cumin, coriander, fenugreek, and oregano)
1 28-ounce can kidney beans
2 cups tomato puree
Salt to taste, if desired
Freshly ground black pepper

1. Sauté the sausage meat until it is lightly browned.
2. Add the garlic and onion and cook ten minutes. Drain off accumulated fat.
3. Add the remaining ingredients and simmer forty-five minutes.

Serves 4.

# Veal and Sausage Stew à la Marsala

*This dish is especially good if prepared a day or two in advance and reheated.*

4 tablespoons vegetable oil
2 tablespoons minced shallots
2 cloves garlic, crushed
12 ounces fresh mushrooms, sliced
1 cup Marsala
¼ cup flour
2 pounds veal, cut into one-inch cubes
1 pound sweet Italian-style sausage, cut into one-inch pieces
2 tablespoons vegetable oil
2 cups beef broth
1 large sweet onion, chopped
1 red and 1 green sweet pepper, cored, seeded, and chopped
2 large potatoes, peeled, and cut into bite-sized pieces
2 cups crushed tomatoes
1 tablespoon dill weed, chopped
½ teaspoon thyme
½ teaspoon oregano
1 tablespoon orange liqueur
1 bay leaf
2 tablespoons flour
¼ cup fresh parsley, chopped
Salt to taste, if desired
Freshly ground black pepper

1. In four tablespoons vegetable oil, sauté the shallots, garlic, and mushrooms until the mushroom liquid evaporates, about ten minutes. Add the Marsala and reduce the liquid by half over high heat. Pour into a three-quart casserole.

2. Dredge the veal in a quarter-cup flour. Sauté the veal and sausages in two tablespoons vegetable oil until they are browned. Add the remaining ingredients, except the parsley and flour. Cook over medium heat for five minutes. Add the remaining flour and stir well.

3. Add this mixture to the casserole and stir.

4. Cover and place in a preheated 350° F oven for one hour. Remove the bay leaf, add the parsley, and serve.

Serves 6 to 8.

## Zucchini Stuffed with Sausage

*It happens every year. We plan, plant, nurture, and sweat over our garden until one day it bursts forth with a bounty of fresh, young, tender vegetables. It also always happens that we eat our fill, put up as much as our pantry shelves and freezer can hold, give away to our neighbors as much as we can before they begin avoiding us, and we still have something left over. More often than not, that something is zucchini. And that's after we've had our fill of fried zucchini, zucchini bread, steamed and buttered zucchini, zucchini pickles, and zucchini this and zucchini that. It's not that we plant too much zucchini, it's just that zucchini vines have a mind of their own, and they don't know when to quit. Consequently, we're always looking for new ways to fix this tasty summer squash. Here is one recipe that you can put to good use when your garden explodes with too much zucchini.*

**2 small to medium zucchini**
**2 pounds bulk sweet Italian sausage**
**¼ cup onion, finely chopped**
**2 cloves garlic, minced**
**¼ pound fresh mushrooms, chopped**
**6 ounces tomato paste**
**¼ cup dry white wine**
**¼ cup grated Romano cheese**
**2 tablespoons fresh parsley, chopped**
**Salt to taste, if desired**
**Freshly ground black pepper**
**Olive oil**

1. In a large pot, boil enough water to cover the zucchini. Add the zucchini to the pot and cook ten minutes. Remove the zucchini, pat dry, and set aside.

2. In a skillet, sauté the sausage until it is lightly browned. Add the onion, garlic, and mushrooms and sauté an additional five minutes. Drain off as much fat as possible and remove from heat.

3. Slice the zucchini in half lengthwise. Scoop out the flesh with a spoon. Be careful not to puncture the skin. Chop the removed flesh and add it to the sausage mixture.

4. Add the tomato paste, wine, cheese, parsley, salt, and pepper. Cook over medium heat five minutes.

5. Place the zucchini halves on a greased baking sheet and divide the sausage mixture between the halves. Sprinkle the Parmesan cheese evenly on top, dribble a little olive oil on each and bake, uncovered, in a preheated 325° F oven for thirty minutes or until the zucchini is tender.

Serves 4.

# Appendix 1

The following is a list of sources for sausage-making supplies. Not all firms carry all the items necessary for making sausage. Most firms will send you a free catalog.

**L. L. Bean, Inc.**
1 Casco Street
Freeport, ME 04033
**207-865-4761**
*Knives, smokers, steamers, smoking chips.*

**Chef's Catalog**
3215 Commercial Avenue
Northbrook, IL 60062
**708-480-9400**
*Grinders, knives, kitchen equipment.*

**China Closet**
7235½ Arlington Road
Falls Church, VA 22042
**703-698-9236**
*Ethnic cooking equipment.*

**Cutlery World**
515 W. 24th Street
New York, NY 10011
**212-924-7300**
*Knives, steels, kitchen shears.*

**DeLaurenti**
1435 First Avenue
Seattle, WA 98101
**206-622-0141**
*Bulk spices.*

**The Forsts**
12-24 Tenbroeck Avenue
Kingston, NY 12401
**914-331-3500**
*Pheasant, partridge, quail, wild turkey, guinea hens, malard ducks.*

**Hammacher Schlemmer**
147 East 57th Street
New York, NY 10022
**212-421-9000**
*Smokers, kitchen equipment.*

**Heartland Sausage Company**
4159 Thomas Avenue North
Minneapolis, MN 55412
**(612) 522-0500**

**Kitchen Bazaar**
1098 Taft Street
Rockville, MD 20850-1308
**301-424-4880**
*Kitchen equipment, knives, grinders.*

**Kitchen Glamor, Inc.**
26770 Grand River
Redford, MI 48240
**313-537-1300**
*Grinders, knives, kitchen equipment.*

**Long Island Beef Co.**
565 West Street
New York, NY 10014
**212-243-1120**
*Venison, game birds, seafood.*

**Manchester Farms**
P.O. Box 97 Highway 521 N.
Dalzell, SC 29040
**803-469-2588**
*Quail.*

**Manganaro Foods**
488 Ninth Avenue
New York, NY 10018
**212-563-5331**
*Sausage funnels, casings, ravioli makers.*

**The Vermont Country Store**
Weston, VT 05161
**802-824-3184**
*Hard to find kitchen equipment.*

**Williams-Sonoma**
100 N. Point St., P.O. Box 7326
San Francisco, CA 94120
**415-617-8690**
*Kitchen equipment and more.*

**Wisconsin Fishing Co.**
P.O. Box 965
Green Bay, WI 54305
**414-437-3582**
*Seafood.*

# Appendix 2

T his is a compendium of sources that you may wish to consult for more information on fat and salt in the human diet, nutrition, and sausage making.

*The Changing American Diet.* Letitia Brewster and Michael Jacobson. Center for Science in the Public Interest, Washington, DC.

*The Complete Sausage Cookbook.* Pamela Riddle and Mary Jane Danley. San Francisco: San Francisco Book Company, 1977.

*Dietary Goals for the United States.* Senate Select Committee on Nutrition and Human Needs. U.S. Government Printing Office, Washington, DC.

*Eating May Be Hazardous to Your Health.* Jacqueline Verrett and Jean Carper. New York: Simon and Schuster, 1974.

*The Food Additives Book.* Nicholas Freydberg and Willis A. Gortner. New York: Bantam Books, 1982.

*Home Made.* Sandra Oddo. New York: Athenaeum, 1972.

*Jane Brody's Nutrition Book.* Jane Brody. New York: W.W. Norton and Co., 1981.

*Junk Food, Fast Food, Health Food.* Lila Perl. New York: Houghton Mifflin Clarion Books, 1980.

*The L.L. Bean Game and Fish Cookbook.* Angus Cameron and Judith Jones. New York: Random House, 1983.

*Nutrition: Concepts and Controversies.* Eva Hamilton and Eleanor Whitney. St. Paul: West Publishing Co., 1979.

*Nature's Kitchen: The Complete Guide to the New American Diet.* Fred Rohé. Vermont: Storey Communications, Inc., Garden Way Publishing, 1986.

# Index

*(continued)*

# Other Storey Books
# You Will Enjoy

**The Canning, Freezing, Curing & Smoking of Meat, Fish & Game,** *by Wilbur F. Eastman, Jr.* A do-it-yourself reference book for those who want to know how to prepare meat, fish, and game so that it can be stored for future use. Text and illustrations combine to answer all your questions. 208 pages. Paperback. ISBN 0-88266-045-4.

**Storey's Guide to Raising Pigs,** *by Kelly Klober.* Covers every aspect of pig raising, including choosing the right breeds, feeding, housing, disease prevention, breeding, butchering, and showing. 320 pages. Paperback. ISBN 1-58017-326-8

**Storey's Guide to Raising Rabbits,** *by Bob Bennett.* Everything for the home and commercial producer. 256 pages. Paperback. ISBN 1-58017-260-1.

**Storey's Guide to Raising Poultry,** *by Leonard Mercia.* In addition to stock selection, brooding, rearing and more, includes current methods of disease prevention and treatment for laying flock, meat chickens, turkeys, ducks, and geese. 352 pages. Paperback. ISBN 1-58017-263-6.

**Storey's Guide to Raising Beef Cattle,** *by Heather Smith Thomas.* Whether you want to raise one or two animals or run a full-scale beef production operation, this book has the information you need. 352 pages. Paperback. ISBN 1-58017-327-6.

**Keeping Livestock Healthy,** *by N. Bruce Haynes, D.V.M* A complete guide to preventing disease through proper housing, good nutrition, and appropriate care. 352 pages. Paperback. ISBN 1-58017-453-3.

**Maple Syrup Cookbook,** *by Ken Haedrich.* More than 100 recipes for every meal, all using maple syrup as the sweetening ingredient. 144 pages. Paperback. ISBN 1-58017-404-3.

**Growing & Using Herbs Successfully,** *by Betty E.M. Jacobs.* Easy growing techniques for 64 herbs, to use in cooking, teas, gifts and medicines. Botanical drawings. 240 pages. Paperback. ISBN 0-88266-249-X.

**Basic Butchering of Livestock & Game,** *by John J. Mettler, Jr., D.V.M.* The only book available on what was once a common practice — easy enough for amateurs, but detailed enough for veterans. It is a book for anyone who hunts, farms, or buys large quantities of meat. How-to drawings. 208 pages. Paperback. ISBN 0-88266-391-7.

*(continued)*

**The Pleasure of Herbs,** *by Phyllis V. Shaudys.* A month-by-month guide to growing, using, and enjoying herbs. Herb enthusiasts will welcome this book because it has gardening tips for each month's featured herb, as well as recipes, an appendix, and all kinds of projects from potpourri mixes to a bridal bouquet. Illustrations, recipes, and charts. 288 pages. Paperback. ISBN 0-88266-423-9.

**Apple Cookbook,** *by Olwen Woodier.* This book shows how to make everything from appetizers and salads to desserts. More than 150 recipes for every meal. Recipes and charts. 176 pages. Paperback. ISBN 1-58017-389-6.

**Build a Smokehouse. Country Wisdom Bulletin A-81.** Included are four smokehouse projects (complete with instructions and material lists) and an explanation of the process by which meat and fish are smoked. 32 pages. Paperback. ISBN 0-88266-295-3.

**These and other Storey books are available at your bookstore, farm store, garden center, or directly from Storey Books, 210 MASS MoCA Way, North Adams, MA 01247, or by calling 1-800-441-5700. Or visit our Web site at www.storey.com.**